Greatest Poetry By Australian Writers

Charles Harpur
Banjo Paterson
Dorothea Mackeller
William Henry Ogilvie
C.J. Dennis
and Others

GRAPEVINE INDIA

Published by

GRAPEVINE INDIA PUBLISHERS PVT LTD

www.grapevineindia.com
Delhi | Mumbai
email: grapevineindiapublishers@gmail.com

Ordering Information:
Quantity sales: Special discounts are available on quantity
purchases by corporations, associations, and others.
For details, reach out to the publisher.

GREATEST POETRY BY AUSTRALIAN WRITERS

CONTENTS

Andy's Gone With Cattle

In The Day's When We Are Dead

Freedom On The Wallaby

The City Bushman

The Song of Australia

The Man from Waterloo (With kind Regards to Banjo)

Dorothea Mackeller

My Country (1908)

The Colours Of Light (1914)

Burning Off (1911)

Fire (1914)

Colour (1914)

An Old Song

The Closed Door

The Witch-Maid

Pilgrim Song

Adam Lindsay Gordon

A Song Of Autumn

The Sick Stockrider

The Swimmer

Wolf And Hound

To My Sister

A Hunting Song

An Exile's Farewell

A Fragment

Henry Kendall

The Last Of His Tribe

Bell Birds

Silent Tears

Bill the Bullock-Driver
The Muse of Australia
Song of the Cattle Hunters
September in Australia
A Mountain Spring

Mary Gilmore
Marri'd

Mary Hannay Foott
Where The Pelican Builds
In The Land Of Dreams
No Message
The Future Of Australia
The Massacre Of The Bards
Happy Days
Up North
To Henry The Fifth
In The South Pacific

John Farrell
Australia
The Last Bullet
Australia To England

Barcroft Boake
Where The Dead Men Lie
Jack's Last Muster
The Demon Snow-Shoes (A Legend of Kiandra)
An Allegory
A Song

C. J. Dennis

The Swagman

The Austra——laise

An Old Master

The Long Road Home

The Triantiwontigongolope

The Looking Glass

The Traveller

William Henry Ogilvie

His Gippsland Girl (1898)

His Epitaph (1898)

The Australian (1916)

From The Gulf

Leila.

A Dreamer Of Dreams.

Ballade Of Windy Nights.

The Cruellest Dream.

Ada Cambridge

Craven-Heart

"After Our Likeness"

"This Enlightened Age"

A Sigh In The Night

CHRISTOPHER BRENNAN

Christopher John Brennan was an Australian poet, scholar, and literary critic. His highly personal verse never was popular with the Australian public but was highly regarded by critics for its vitality and sincerity. Much of his work was virtually unobtainable for many years, having originally been produced in small editions or circulated privately in typescript. A collected edition in 1958 helped rescue his reputation from obscurity. His verse shows the influence of Greek and Latin poets. Brennan influenced Australian writers of his generation and many who succeeded him.

BECAUSE SHE WOULD ASK ME WHY I LOVED HER

If questioning would make us wise
No eyes would ever gaze in eyes;
If all our tale were told in speech
No mouths would wander each to each.

Were spirits free from mortal mesh
And love not bound in hearts of flesh
No aching breasts would yearn to meet
And find their ecstasy complete.

For who is there that lives and knows
The secret powers by which he grows?
Were knowledge all, what were our need
To thrill and faint and sweetly bleed?

Then seek not, sweet, the "If" and "Why"
I love you now until I die.
For I must love because I live
And life in me is what you give.

AUTUMN

Autumn: the year breathes dully towards its death,
beside its dying sacrificial fire;
the dim world's middle-age of vain desire
is strangely troubled, waiting for the breath
that speaks the winter's welcome malison
to fix it in the unremembering sleep:
the silent woods brood o'er an anxious deep,
and in the faded sorrow of the sun,
I see my dreams' dead colours, one by one,
forth-conjur'd from their smouldering palaces,
fade slowly with the sigh of the passing year.
They wander not nor wring their hands nor weep,
discrown'd belated dreams! but in the drear
and lingering world we sit among the trees
and bow our heads as they, with frozen mouth,
looking, in ashen reverie, towards the clear
sad splendour of the winter of the far south.

THE WANDERER

When window-lamps had dwindled, then I rose
and left the town behind me; and on my way
passing a certain door I stopt, remembering
how once I stood on its threshold, and my life
was offer'd to me, a road how different
from that of the years since gone! and I had but
to rejoin an olden path, once dear, since left.
All night I have walk'd and my heart was deep awake,
remembering ways I dream'd and that I chose,
remembering luridly, and was not sad,
being brimm'd with all the liquid and clear dark
of the night that was not stirr'd with any tide;
for leaves were silent and the road gleam'd pale,
following the ridge, and I was alone with night.
But now 1 am come among the rougher hills
and grow aware of the sea that somewhere near
is restless; and the flood of night is thinn'd
and stars are whitening. 0, what horrible dawn
will bare me the way and crude lumps of the hills
and the homeless concave of the day, and bare
the ever-restless, ever-complaining sea?

Each day I see the long ships coming into port
and the people crowding to their rail, glad of the shore:
because to have been alone with the sea and not to have known
of anything happening in any crowded way,
and to have heard no other voice than the crooning sea's
has charmed away the old rancours, and the great winds
have search'd and swept their hearts of the old irksome thoughts:
so, to their freshen'd gaze, each land smiles a good home.
Why envy I, seeing them made gay to greet the shore?

Surely I do not foolishly desire to go
hither and thither upon the earth and grow weary
with seeing many lands and peoples and the sea:
but if I might, some day, landing I reck not where
have heart to find a welcome and perchance a rest,
I would spread the sail to any wandering wind of the air
this night, when waves are hard and rain blots out the land

I am driven everywhere from a clinging home,
0 autumn eves! and I ween'd that you would yet
have made, when your smouldering dwindled to odorous fume,
close room for my heart, where I might crouch and dream
of days and ways I had trod, and look with regret
on the darkening homes of men and the window-gleam,
and forget the morrows that threat and the unknown way.
But a bitter wind came out of the yellow-pale west
and my heart is shaken and fill'd with its triumphing cry:
You shall find neither home nor rest: for ever you roam
with stars as they drift and wilful fates of the sky!

0 tame heart, and why are you weary and cannot rest?
here is the hearth with its glow and the roof that forbids the rain,
a swept and a garnish'd quiet, a peace: and were you not fain
to be gather'd in dusk and comfort and barter away the rest ?

And is your dream now of riding away from a stricken field
on a lost and baleful eve, when the world went out in rain,
one of some few that rode evermore by the bridle-rein
of a great beloved chief, with high heart never to yield?

Was that you? and you ween you are back in your life of old
when you dealt as your pride allow'd and reck'd not of other rein?

Nay, tame heart, be not idle: it is but the ardent rain
that minds you of manhood foregone and the perilous joy of the bold

Once I could sit by the fire hourlong when the dripping caves
sang cheer to the shelterd, and listen, and know that the woods drank fig
and think of the morn that was coming and how the freshen'd leaves
would glint in the sun and the dusk beneath would be bright and cool.

Now, when I hear, I am cold within: for my mind drifts wide
where the blessing is shed for naught on the salt waste of the sea,
on the valleys that hold no rest and the hills that may not abide:
and the fire loses its warmth and my home is far from me.

How old is my heart, how old, how old is my heart,
and did I ever go forth with song when the morn was new?
I seem to have trod on many ways: I seem to have left
I know not how many homes; and to leave each
was still to leave a portion of mine own heart,
of my old heart whose life I had spent to make that home
and all I had was regret, and a memory.
So I sit and muse in this wayside harbour and wait
till I hear the gathering cry of the ancient winds and again
I must up and out and leave the embers of the hearth
to crumble silently into white ash and dust,
and see the road stretch bare and pale before me: again
my garment and my home shall be the enveloping winds
and my heart be fill'd wholly with their old pitiless cry.

I sorrow for youth - ah, not for its wildness (would that were dead!)
but for those soft nests of time that enticed the maiden bloom
of delight and tenderness to break in delicate air
- 0 her eyes in the rosy face that bent over our first babe!

but all that was, and is gone, and shall be all forgotten;
it fades and wanes even now: and who is there cares but I?
and I grieve for my heart that is old and cannot cease from regret.
Ay, might our harms be haven'd in some deathless heart:
but where have I felt its over-brooding luminous tent
save in those eyes of delight (and ah! that they must change)
and of yore in her eyes to whom we ran with our childish joy?
0 brother! if such there were and each of us might lead each
to lean above the little pools where all our heart
lies spilt and clear and shining along the dusky way,
and dream of one that could save it all and salve our ache!

You, at whose table I have sat, some distant eve
beside the road, and eaten and you pitied me
to be driven an aimless way before the pitiless winds,
how much ye have given and knew not, pitying foolishly!
For not alone the bread I broke, but I tasted too
all your unwitting lives and knew the narrow soul
that bodies it in the landmarks of your fields,
and broods dumbly within your little season:? round,
where, after sowing, comes the short-lived sunune?s mirth,
and, after harvesting, the winter's lingering dream,
half memory and,regret, half hope, crouching beside
the hearth that is your only centre of life and dream.
And knowing the world how limitless and the way how long,
and, the home of man how feeble and builded on the winds,
I have lived your life, that eve, as you might never live
knowing, and pity you, if you should come to know.

I cry to you as I pass your windows in the dusk;
Ye have built you unmysterious homes and ways in the wood
where of old ye went with sudden eyes to the right and left;

and your going was now made safe and your staying comforted,
for the forest edge itself, holding old savagery
in unsearch'd glooms, was your houses' friendly barrier.
And now that the year goes winterward, ye thought to hide
behind your gleaming panes, and where the hearth sings merrily
make cheer with meat and wine, and sleep in the long night,
and the uncared wastes might be a crying unhappiness.
But I, who have come from the outer night, I say to you
the winds are up and terribly will they shake the dry wood:
the woods shall awake, hearing them, shall awake to be toss'd and riven,
and make a cry and a parting in your sleep all night
as the wither'd leaves go whirling all night along all ways.
And when ye come forth at dawn, uncomforted by sleep,
ye shall stand at amaze, beholding all the ways overhidden
with worthless drift of the dead and all your broken world:
and ye shall not know whence the winds have come, nor shall ye know
whither the yesterdays have fled, or if they were.

Come out, come out, ye souls that serve, why will ye die?
or will ye sit and stifle in your prison-homes
dreaming of some master that holds the winds in leash
and the waves of darkness yonder in the gaunt hollow of night?
nay, there is none that rules: all is a strife of the winds
and the night shall billow in storm full oft ere all be done.
For this is the hard doom that is laid on all of you,
to be that whereof ye dream, dreaming against your will.
But first ye must travel the many ways, and your close-wrapt souls
must be blown thro' with the rain that comes from the homeless dark:
for until ye have had care of the wastes there shall be no truce
for them nor you, nor home, but ever the ancient feud;
and the soul of man must house the cry of the darkling waves
as he follows the ridge above the waters shuddering towards night,

and the rains and the winds that roam anhunger'd for some heart's warmth.

Go: tho' ye find it bitter, yet must ye be bare

to the wind and the sea and the night and the wail of birds in the sky;

go: tho' the going be hard and the goal blinded with rain

yet the staying is a death that is never soften'd with sleep

Dawns of the world, how I have known you all,

so many, and so varied, and the same!

dawns o'er the timid plains, or in the folds

of the arm'd hills, or by the unsleeping shore;

a chill touch on the chill flesh of the dark

that, shuddering, shrinks from its couch, and leaves

a homeless light, staring, disconsolate,

on the drear world it knows too well, the world

it fled and finds again, its wistful hope

unmet by any miracle of night,

that mocks it rather, with its shreds that hang

about the woods and huddled bulks of gloom

that crouch, malicious, in the broken combes,

witness to foulnesses else unreveal'd

that visit earth and violate her dreams

in the lone hours when only evil wakes.

What is there with you and me, that I may not forget

but your white shapes come crowding noiselessly in my nights,

making my sleep a flight from a thousand beckoning hands?

Was it not enough that your cry dwelt in my waking ears

that now, seeking oblivion, I must yet be haunted

by cach black maw of hunger that yawns despairingly

a moment ere its whitening frenzy bury it?

0 waves of all the seas, would I could give you peace

and find my peace again: for all my peace is fled

and broken and blown along your white delirious crests!

0 desolate eves along the way, how oft,
despite your bitterness, was I warm at heart!
not with the glow of rememberd hearths, but warm
with the solitary unquenchable fire that bums
a flameless heat deep in his heart who has come
where the formless winds plunge and exult for aye
among the naked spaces of the world,
far past the circle of the ruddy hearths
and all their memories. Desperate eves,
when the wind-bitten hills tum'd violet
along their rims, and the earth huddled her heat
within her ****rd bosom, and the dead stones
lay battle-strewn before the iron wind
that, blowing from the chill west, made all its way
a loneliness to yield its triumph room;
yet in that wind a clamour of trumpets rang,
old trumpets, resolute, stark, undauntable,
singing to battle against the eternal foe,
the wronger of this world, and all his powers
in some last fight, foredoom'd disastrous,
upon the final ridges of the world:
a war-wom note, stem fire in the stricken eve,
and fire thro' all my ancient heart, that sprang
towards that last hope of a glory won in defeat,
whence, knowing not sure if such high grace befall
at the end, yet I draw courage to front the way.

The land I came thro' last was dumb with night,
a limbo of defeated glory, a ghost:
for wreck of constellations flickerd perishing

scarce sustained in the mortuary air,

and on the ground and out of livid pools

wreck of old swords and crowns glimmer'd at whiles;

I seem'd at home in some old dream of kingship:

now it is clear grey day and the road is plain,

I am the wanderer of many years

who cannot tell if ever he was king

or if ever kingdoms were: I know I am

the wanderer of the ways of all the worlds,

to whom the sunshine and the rain are one

and one to stay or hasten, because he knows

no ending of the way, no home, no goal,

and phantom night and the grey day alike

withhold the heart where all my dreams and days

might faint in soft fire and delicious death:

and saying this to myself as a simple thing

I feel a peace fall in the heart of the winds

and a clear dusk settle, somewhere, far in me.

THIS MISERY MUST END

I said, This misery must end:
Shall I, that am a man and know
that sky and wind are yet my friend,
sit huddled under any blow?
so speaking left the dismal room
and stept into the mother-night
all fill'd with sacred quickening gloom
where the few stars burn'd low and bright,
and darkling on my darkling hill
heard thro' the beaches' sullen boom
heroic note of living will
rung trumpet-clear against the fight;
so stood and heard, and rais'd my eyes
erect, that they might drink of space,
and took the night upon my face,
till time and trouble fell away
and all my soul sprang up to feel
as one among the stars that reel
in rhyme on their rejoicing way,
breaking the elder dark, nor stay
but speed beyond each trammelling gyre,
till time and sorrow fall away
and night be wither'd up, and fire
consume the sickness of desire.

I AM SHUT OUT OF MINE OWN HEART

I am shut out of mine own heart
because my love is far from me,
nor in the wonders have I part
that fill its hidden empery:

the wildwood of adventurous thought
and lands of dawn my dream had won,
the riches out of Faery brought
are buried with our bridal sun.

And I am in a narrow place,
and all its little streets are cold,
because the absence of her face
has robb'd the sullen air of gold.

My home is in a broader day:
at times I catch it glistening
thro' the dull gate, a flower'd play
and odour of undying spring:

the long days that I lived alone,
sweet madness of the springs I miss'd,
are shed beyond, and thro' them blown
clear laughter, and my lips are kiss'd:

- and here, from mine own joy apart,
I wait the turning of the key: -
I am shut out of mine own heart
because my love is far from me.

FIRE IN THE HEAVENS

Fire in the heavens, and fire along the hills,
and fire made solid in the flinty stone,
thick-mass'd or scatter'd pebble, fire that fills
the breathless hour that lives in fire alone.

This valley, long ago the patient bed
of floods that carv'd its antient amplitude,
in stillness of the Egyptian crypt outspread,
endures to drown in noon-day's tyrant mood.

Behind the veil of burning silence bound,
vast life's innumerous busy littleness
is hush'd in vague-conjectured blur of sound
that dulls the brain with slumbrous weight, unless

some dazzling puncture let the stridence throng
in the cicada's torture-point of song.

SPRING BREEZES

Spring breezes over the blue,
now lightly frolicking in some tropic bay,
go forth to meet her way,
for here the spell hath won and dream is true.

0 happy wind, thou that in her warm hair
mayst rest and play!
could I but breathe all longing into thee,
so were thy viewless wing
as flame or thought, hastening her shining way.

And now I bid thee bring
tenderly hither over a subject sea
that golden one whose grace hath made me king,
and, soon to glad my gaze at shut of day,
loosen'd in happy air
her charmed hair.

SWEET SILENCE AFTER BELLS

Sweet silence after bells!
deep in the enamour'd ear
soft incantation dwells.

Filling the rapt still sphere
a liquid crystal swims,
precarious yet clear.

Those metal quiring hymns
shaped ether so succinct:
a while, or it dislimns,

the silence, wanly prinkt
with forms of lingering notes,
inhabits, close. distinct;

and night, the angel, floats
on wings of blessing spread
o'er all the gather'd cotes

where meditation, wed
with love, in gold-lit cells,
absorbs the heaven that shed

sweet silence after bells.

CHARLES HARPUR

Charles Harpur was an Australian poet and playwright. He is regarded as "Australia's most important nineteenth-century poet," best known for poems on Australian themes that use traditional English poetic forms. Many of Harpur's poems describe the Australian bush. Scholars have praised the accuracy and variety of his natural descriptions while critiquing his tendency to 'Gothicise' the Australian landscape. Harpur underpinned his nature poetry with a sophisticated theory of natural description.

A MIDSUMMER NOON IN THE AUSTRALIAN FOREST

Not a bird disturbs the air!
There is quiet everywhere;
Over plains and over woods
What a mighty stillness broods.

Even the grasshoppers keep
[All the birds and insects keep]
Where the coolest shadows sleep;
Even the busy ants are found
Resting in their pebbled mound;
Even the locust clingeth now
In silence to the barky bough:
And over hills and over plains
Quiet, vast and slumbrous, reigns.

Only there's a drowsy humming
From yon warm lagoon slow coming:
'Tis the dragon-hornet - see!
All bedaubed resplendently
With yellow on a tawny ground -
Each rich spot nor square nor round,
But rudely heart-shaped, as it were
The blurred and hasty impress there,
Of vermeil-crusted seal
Dusted o'er with golden meal:
Only there's a droning where
Yon bright beetle gleams the air -
Gleams it in its droning flight
[Tracks it in its gleaming flight]
With a slanting track of light,

Till rising in the sunshine higher,
[Rising in the sunshine higher,]
Its shards flame out like gems on fire.
[Till its shards flame out like fire.]

Every other thing is still,
Save the ever wakeful rill,
Whose cool murmur only throws
A cooler comfort round Repose;
Or some ripple in the sea
Of leafy boughs, where, lazily,
Tired Summer, in her forest bower
Turning with the noontide hour,
Heaves a slumbrous breath, ere she
Once more slumbers peacefully.

0 'tis easeful here to lie
Hidden from Noon's scorching eye,
In this grassy cool recess
Musing thus of Quietness.

THE CREEK OF THE FOUR GRAVES
[LATE VERSION]

PART I.

A settler in the olden times went forth
With four of his most bold and trusted men
Into the wilderness—went forth to seek
New streams and wider pastures for his fast
Increasing flocks and herds. O'er mountain routes
And over wild wolds clouded up with brush,
And cut with marshes perilously deep,—
So went they forth at dawn; at eve the sun,
That rose behind them as they journeyed out,
Was firing with his nether rim a range
Of unknown mountains, that like ramparts towered
Full in their front. and his last glances fell
Into the gloomy forest's eastern glades
In golden gleams, like to the Angel's sword,
And flashed upon the windings of a creek
That noiseless ran betwixt the pioneers
And those new Apennines—ran, shaded o'er
With boughs of the wild willow, hanging mixed
From either-bank, or duskily befringed
With upward tapering feathery swamp-oaks,
The sylvan eyelash always of remote
Australian waters, whether gleaming still
In lake or pool, or bickering along,
Between the marges of some eager stream.
Before them, thus extended, wilder grew
The scene each moment and more beautiful;
For when the sun was all but sunk below
Those barrier mountains, in the breeze that o'er

Their rough enormous backs deep-fleeced with wood
Came whispering down, the wide up-slanting sea
Of fanning leaves in the descending rays
Danced dazzlingly, tingling as if the trees
Thrilled to the roots for very happiness.

But when the sun had wholly disappeared
Behind those mountains—O what words, what hues
Might paint the wild magnificence of view
That opened westward! Out extending, lo!
The heights rose crowding, with their summits all
Dissolving as it seemed, and partly lost
In the exceeding radiancy aloft;
And thus transfigured, for awhile they stood
Like a great company of archaeons, crowned
With burning diadems, and tented o'er
With canopies of purple and of gold.

Here halting wearied now the sun was set,
Our travellers kindled for their first night's camp
A brisk and crackling fire, which seemed to them,
A wilder creature than 'twas elsewhere wont,
Because of the surrounding savageness.
And as they supped, birds of new shape and plume
And wild strange voice came by; and up the steep
Between the climbing forest growths they saw
Perched on the bare abutments of the hills,
Where haply yet some lingering gleam fell through,
The wallaroo look forth. Eastward at last
The glow was wasted into formless gloom,
Night's front; then westward the high massing woods
Steeped in a swart but mellow Indian hue,

A deep dusk loveliness, lay ridged and heaped,
Only the more distinctly for their shade,
Against the twilight hearen—a cloudless depth,
Yet luminous with sunset's fading glow;
And thus awhile in the lit dusk they seemed
To hang like mighty pictures of themselves
In the still chambers of some vaster world.

At last, the business of the supper done,
The echoes of the solitary place
Came as in sylvan wonder wide about
To hear and imitate the voices strange,
Within the pleasant purlieus of the fire
Lifted in glee; but to be hushed erelong,
As with the darkness of the night there came
O'er the adventurers, each and all, some sense
Of danger lurking in its forest lairs.

But, nerved by habit, they all gathered round
About the well-built fire, whose nimble tongues
Sent up continually a strenuous roar
Of fierce delight, and from their fuming pipes
Drawing rude comfort, round the pleasant light
With grave discourse they planned their next day's deeds.
Wearied at length, their couches they prepared
Of rushes, and the long green tresses pulled
From the bent boughs of the wild willows near;
Then the four men stretched out their tired limbs
Under the dark arms of the forest trees
That mixed aloft, high in the starry air,
In arcs and leafy domes whose crossing curves,
Blended with denser intergrowth of sprays,

Were seen, in mass traced out against the clear

Wide gaze of heaven; and trustful of the watch

Kept near them by their master, soon they slept,

Forgetful of the perilous wilderness

That lay around them like a spectral world;

And all things slept; the circling forest trees,

Their foremost boles carved from a crowded mass

Less visible by the watch-fire's bladed gleams

That ran far out in the umbrageous dark

Beyond the broad red ring of constant light;

And, even the shaded mountains darkly seen,

Their bluff brows looming through the stirless air,

Looked in their stillness solemnly asleep:

Yea, thence surveyed, the universe might have seemed

Coiled in vast rest;—only that one dark cloud,

Diffused and shapen like a spider huge,

Crept as with scrawling legs along the sky

And that the stars in their bright orders, still

Cluster by cluster glowingly revealed,

As this slow cloud moved on, high over all,

Peaceful and wakeful, watched the world below.

PART II.

Meanwhile the cloudless eastern heaven had grown
More luminous, and now the moon arose
Above the hill, when lo! that giant cone
Erewhile so dark, seemed inwardly aglow
With her instilled irradiance, while the trees
That fringed its outline, their huge statures dwarfed
By distance into brambles and yet all
Clearly defined against her ample orb,
Out of its very disc appeared to swell
In shadowy relief, as they had been
All sculptured from its surface as she rose.
Then her full light in silvery sequence still
Cascading forth from ridgy slope to slope,
Chased mass by mass the broken darkness down
Into the dense-brushed valleys, where it crouched,
And shrank, and struggled, like a dragon-doubt
Glooming a lonely spirit.

His lone watch
The master kept, and wakeful looked abroad
On all the solemn beauty of the world;
And by some sweet and subtle tie that joins
The loved and cherished, absent from our side,
With all that is serene and beautiful
In Nature, thoughts of home began to steal
Into his musings—when, on a sudden, hark!
A bough cracks loudly in a neighbouring brake!
Against the shade-side of a bending gum.
With a strange horror gathering to his heart,
As if his blood were charged with insect life
And writhed along in clots, he stilled himself

And listened heedfully, till his held breath
Became a pang. Nought heard he: silence there
Had recomposed her ruffled wings, and now
Deep brooded in the darkness; so that he
Again mused on, quiet and reassured.

But there again—crack upon crack! Awake!
O heaven! have hell's worst fiends burst howling up
Into the death-doomed world? Or whence, if not
From diabolic rage, could surge a yell
So horrible as that which now affrights
The shuddering dark! Beings as fell are near!
Yea, beings in their dread inherited hate
Awful, vengeful as hell's worst fiends, are come
In vengeance! For behold from the long grass
And nearer brakes arise the bounding forms
Of painted savages, full in the light
Thrown outward by the fire, that roused and lapped.
The rounding darknesswith its ruddy tongues
More fiercely than before, as though even it
Had felt the sudden shock the air received
From those terrific cries.

On then they came
And rushed upon the sleepers, three of whom
But started, and then weltered prone beneath
The first fell blow dealt down on each by three
Of the most stalwart of their pitiless foes
But one again, and yet again, rose up,
Rose to his knees, under the crushing strokes
Of huge clubbed nulla-nullas, till his own
Warm blood was blinding him. For he was one

Who had with misery nearly all his days
Lived lonely, and who therefore in his soul
Did hunger after hope, and thirst for what
Hope still had promised him, some taste at least
Of human good however long deferred.
And now he could not, even in dying, loose
His hold on life's poor chances still to come,
Could not but so dispute the terrible fact
Of death, e'en in death's presence. Strange it is,
Yet oft 'tis seen, that fortune's pampered child
Consents to death's untimely power with less
Reluctance, less despair, than does the wretch
Who hath been ever blown about the world,
The straw-like sport of fate's most bitter blasts
So though the shadows of untimely death,
Inevitably under every stroke
But thickened more and more, against them still
The poor wretch struggled, nor would cease until
One last great blow, dealt down upon his head
As if in mercy, gave him to the dust,
With all his many woes and frustrate hopes.

The master, chilled with horror, saw it all;
From instinct more than conscious thought he raised
His death-charged tube, and at that murderous crew
Firing, saw one fall ox-like to the earth,
Then turned and fled. Fast fled he, but as fast
His deadly foes went thronging on his track.
Fast! for in full pursuit behind him yelled
Men whose wild speech no word for mercy hath!
And as he fled the forest beasts as well
In general terror through the brakes ahead

Crashed scattering, or with maddening speed athwart

His course came frequent. On, still on, he flies—

Flies for dear life, and still behind him hears

Nearer and nearer, the light rapid dig ,

Of many feet—nearer and nearer still.

PART III.

So went the chase. Now at a sudden turn
Before him lay the steep-banked mountain creek;
Still on he kept perforce, and from a rock
That beaked the bank, a promontory bare,
Plunging right forth and shooting feet-first down,
Sunk to his middle in the flashing stream,
In which the imaged stars seemed all at once
To burst like rockets into one wide blaze.
Then wading through the ruffled waters, forth
He sprang, and seized a snake-like root that from
The opponent bank protruded, clenching there
His cold hand like a clamp of steel; and thence
He swung his dripping form aloft, the blind
And breathless haste of one who flies for life
Urging him on; up the dark ledge he climbed,
When in its face—O verily our God
Hath those in His peculiar care, for whom
The daily prayers of spotless womanhood
And helpless infancy are offered up!
There in its face a cavity he felt,
The upper earth of which in one rude mass
Was held fast bound by the enwoven roots
Of two old trees, and which, beneath the mould,
Over the dark and clammy cave below,
Twisted like knotted snakes.
'Neath these he crept,
Just as the dark forms of his hunters thronged
The steep bold rock whence he before had plunged.

Duskily visible beneath the moon
They paused a space, to mark what bent his course

Might take beyond the stream. But now no form
Amongst the moveless fringe of fern was seen
To shoot up from its outline, 'mid the boles
And mixing shadows of the taller trees,
All standing now in the keen radiance there
So ghostly still as in a solemn trance;
But nothing in the silent prospect stirred
Therefore they augured that their prey was yet
Within the nearer distance, and they all
Plunged forward till the fretted current boiled
Amongst their crowding forms from bank to bank
And searching thus the stream across, and then
Along the ledges, combing down each clump
Of long-flagged swamp-grass where it flourished high,
The whole dark line passed slowly, man by man,
Athwart the cave!

Keen was their search but vain,
There grouped in dark knots standing in the stream
That glimmered past them moaning as it went,
They marvelled; passing strange to them it seemed
Some old mysterious fable of their race,
That brooded o'er the valley and the creek,
Returned upon their minds, and fear-struck all
And silent, they withdrew. And when the sound
Of their retreating steps had died away,
As back they hurried to despoil the dead
In the stormed camp, then rose the fugitive,
Renewed his flight, nor rested from it, till
He gained the shelter of his longed-for home.
And in that glade, far in the doomful wild,
In sorrowing record of an awful hour

Of human agony and loss extreme,
Untimely spousals with a desert death,
Four grassy mounds are there beside the creek,
Bestrewn with sprays and leaves from the old trees
Which moan the ancient dirges that have caught
The heed of dying ages, and for long
The traveller passing then in safety there
Would call the place—The Creek of the Four Graves.

AN ABORIGINAL MOTHER'S LAMENT: EARLY VERSION

Still farther would I fly, my child,
To make thee safer yet,
From the unsparing white man,
With his dread hand murder-wet!
I'll bear thee on as I have borne
With stealthy steps wind-fleet,
But the dark night shrouds the forest,
And thorns are in my feet.
O moan not! I would give this braid—
Thy father's gift to me—
But for a single palmful
Of water now for thee.

Ah! Spring not to his name—no more
To glad us may he come!
He is smouldering into ashes
Beneath the blasted gum!
All charred and blasted by the fire
The white man kindled there,
And fed with our slaughtered kindred
Till heaven-high went its glare!

O moan not! I would give this braid—
Thy father's gift to me—
For but a single palmful
Of water now for thee.

And but for thee, I would their fire
Had eaten me as fast!
Hark! Hark! I hear his death-cry

Yet lengthening up the blast!
But no—when that we should fly,
On the roaring pyre flung bleeding—
I saw thy father die!

O moan not! I would give this braid—
Thy father's gift to me—
For but a single palmful
Of water now for thee.

No more shall his loud tomahawk
Be plied to win our cheer,
Or the shining fish-pools darken
Beneath his shadowing spear;
The fading tracks of his fleet foot
Shall guide not as before,
And the mountain-spirits mimic
His hunting call no more!

O moan not! I would give this braid—
Thy father's gift to me—
For but a single palmful
Of water now for thee.

THE BATTLE OF LIFE

Never give up, though life be a battle
Wherein true men may fail, and true causes be sold;
Yet, on the whole, however may rattle
The thunders of chance, scaring cowards like cattle—
Clear victory's always the bride of the bold.
Armed in your right-though friendship deny you,
And love fall away when the storm's at the worst,
Count not your loss, Was destined to try you—
Bear the brunt like a man, and your deeds shall ally you
To natures more noble and true than the first.

Rail not at Fate: if rightly you scan her,
There's none loves more strongly the heart that endures:
On, in the hero's calm resolute manner,
Still bear aloft your hope's long-trusted banner,
And the day, if you do but live through it, is yours.

Be this your faith; and if killing strokes clatter
On your harness where true men before you have died,
Fight on, let your life-blood be poured out like water—
Fight on, make at least a brave end of the matter,
Brave end of the struggle if nothing beside

A BASKET OF SUMMER FRUIT

First see those ample melons-brindled o'er
With mingled green and brown is all the rind;
For they are ripe, and mealy at the core,
And saturate with the nectar of their kind.

And here their fellows of the marsh are set,
Covering their sweetness with a crumpled skin;
Pomegranates next, flame-red without, and yet
With vegetable crystals stored within.

Then mark these brilliant oranges, of which
A by-gone Poet fancifully said,
Their unplucked globes the orchard did enrich
Like Lolden lamps in a green nilht of shade.

With these are lemons that are even more
Golden than they, and which adorn our Rhyme,
As did rough pendants of barbaric ore
Some pillared temple of the olden time.

And here are peaches with their ruddy cheeks
And ripe transparency. Here nectarines bloom,
All mottled as with discontinuous streaks.
And spread a fruity fragrance through the room.

With these are cherries mellow to the stone;
Into such ripeness bath the summer nursed them,
The velvet pressure of the tongue alone
Against the palate were enough to burst them.

Here too are plums, like edible rubies glowing -

The language of lush summer's Eden theme:
Even through the skin how temptingly keeps showing
Their juicy comfort, a rich-clouded gleam!

Here too are figs, pears, apples (plucked in haste
Our summer treat judiciously to vary)
With apricots, so exquisite in taste,
And yellow as the breast of a canary.

And luscious strawberries all faceted
With glittering lobes-and all the lovelier seen
In contrast with the loquat's duller red,
And vulgar gooseberry's unlustrous green.

And lastly, bunches of rich blooded grapes
Whose vineyard bloom even yet about them clings.
Though ever in the handling it escapes
Like the fine down upon a moth's bright wings.

Each kind is piled in order in the Basket,
Which we might well imagine now to be
Transmuted into a great golden casket
Entreasuring Pomona's jewelry.

THIS SOUTHERN LAND OF OURS

With alien hearts to frame our laws
And cheat us as of old,
In vain our soil is rich, in vain
'Tis seamed with virgin gold:
But the present only yields us nought,
The future only lours
Till we dare to be a people
In this Southern Land of Ours.

What would pygmean statesmen but
Our new-world prospects blast,
By chaining native enterprise
To Europe's pauper past,
With all its misery for the mass,
And fraud-upholden powers;
But we'll yet have men, - like Cromwell,
In this Southern Land of Ours.

And lo, the unploughed future, boys,
May yet be all our own,
If hearts that love their Native Land
Determine this alone:
To sow its years with crops of truth,
And border these with flowers,
Till we have a birth of heroes
In this Southern Land of Ours.

BANJO PATERSON

Andrew Barton "Banjo" Paterson, CBE, was an Australian bush poet, journalist, and author. He wrote many ballads and poems about Australian life, focusing mainly on the rural and outback areas, including the district around Binalong, New South Wales, where he spent much of his childhood. He achieved widespread success in Australia with The Man from Snowy River and Other Verses (1895), which sold more than 100,000 copies before his death, and Rio Grande's Last Race and Other Verses (1902), which also went through many editions. His poem "Waltzing Matilda," published in 1895, is regarded widely as Australia's unofficial national anthem.

WALTZING MATILDA

Oh there once was a swagman camped in the billabong,
Under the shade of a Coolabah tree;
And he sang as he looked at his old billy boiling
"Who'll come a-waltzing Matilda with me."

Who'll come a-waltzing Matilda, my darling.
Who'll come a-waltzing Matilda with me.
Waltzing Matilda and leading a water-bag —
Who'll come a-waltzing Matilda with me.

Down came a jumbuck to drink at the waterhole,
Up jumped the swagman and grabbed him in glee;
And he sang as he stowed him away in his tucker-bag,
"You'll come a-waltzing Matilda with me."

Who'll come a-waltzing Matilda, my darling.
Who'll come a-waltzing Matilda with me.
Waltzing Matilda and leading a water-bag —
Who'll come a-waltzing Matilda with me.

Down came the squatter a-riding his thoroughbred;
Down came policemen — one, two, and three.
"Whose is the jumbuck you've got in the tucker-bag?
You'll come a-waltzing Matilda with we."

Who'll come a-waltzing Matilda, my darling.
Who'll come a-waltzing Matilda with me.
Waltzing Matilda and leading a water-bag —
Who'll come a-waltzing Matilda with me.

But the swagman, he up and he jumped in the waterhole,

Drowning himself by the Coolabah tree;
And his ghost may be heard as it sings in the billabong
"Who'll come a-waltzing Matilda with me?"

Who'll come a-waltzing Matilda, my darling.
Who'll come a-waltzing Matilda with me.
Waltzing Matilda and leading a water-bag.
Who'll come a-waltzing Matilda with me.

THE MAN FROM SNOWY RIVER

There was movement at the station, for the word had passed around
  That the colt from Old Regret had got away,
And had joined the wild bush horses - he was worth a thousand pound,
  So all the cracks had gathered to the fray.
All the tried and noted riders from the stations near and far
  Had mustered at the homestead overnight,
For the bushmen love hard riding where the wild bush horses are,
  And the stock-horse snuffs the battle with delight.

There was Harrison, who made his pile when Pardon won the cup,
  The old man with his hair as white as snow;
But few could ride beside him when his blood was fairly up —
  He would go wherever horse and man could go.
And Clancy of the Overflow came down to lend a hand,
  No better horseman ever held the reins;
For never horse could throw him while the saddle girths would stand,
  He learnt to ride while droving on the plains.

And one was there, a stripling on a small and weedy beast;
  He was something like a racehorse undersized,
With a touch of Timor pony — three parts thoroughbred at least —
  And such as are by mountain horsemen prized.
He was hard and tough and wiry — just the sort that won't say die —
  There was courage in his quick impatient tread;
And he bore the badge of gameness in his bright and fiery eye,
  And the proud and lofty carriage of his head.

But still so slight and weedy, one would doubt his power to stay,
  And the old man said, "That horse will never do
For a long and tiring gallop - lad, you'd better stop away,
  Those hills are far too rough for such as you."

So he waited sad and wistful — only Clancy stood his friend —
"I think we ought to let him come," he said;
"I warrant he'll be with us when he's wanted at the end,
For both his horse and he are mountain bred."

"He hails from Snowy River, up by Kosciusko's side,
Where the hills are twice as steep and twice as rough,
Where a horse's hoofs strike firelight from the flint stones every stride,
The man that holds his own is good enough.
And the Snowy River riders on the mountains make their home,
Where the river runs those giant hills between;
I have seen full many horsemen since I first commenced to roam,
But nowhere yet such horsemen have I seen."

So he went; they found the horses by the big mimosa clump,
They raced away towards the mountain's brow,
And the old man gave his orders, "Boys, go at them from the jump,
No use to try for fancy riding now.
And, Clancy, you must wheel them, try and wheel them to the right.
Ride boldly, lad, and never fear the spills,
For never yet was rider that could keep the mob in sight,
If once they gain the shelter of those hills."

So Clancy rode to wheel them — he was racing on the wing
Where the best and boldest riders take their place,
And he raced his stockhorse past them, and he made the ranges ring
With the stockwhip, as he met them face to face.
Then they halted for a moment, while he swung the dreaded lash,
But they saw their well-loved mountain full in view,
And they charged beneath the stockwhip with a sharp and sudden dash,
And off into the mountain scrub they flew.

Then fast the horsemen followed, where the gorges deep and black
Resounded to the thunder of their tread,
And the stockwhips woke the echoes, and they fiercely answered back
From cliffs and crags that beetled overhead.
And upward, ever upward, the wild horses held their way,
Where Mountain Ash and Kurrajong grew wide;
And the old man muttered fiercely, "We may bid the mob good day,
No man can hold them down the other side."

When they reached the mountain's summit, even Clancy took a pull -
It well might make the boldest hold their breath;
The wild hop scrub grew thickly, and the hidden ground was full
Of wombat holes, and any slip was death.
But the man from Snowy River let the pony have his head,
And he swung his stockwhip round and gave a cheer,
And he raced him down the mountain like a torrent down its bed,
While the others stood and watched in very fear.

He sent the flint-stones flying, but the pony kept his feet,
He cleared the fallen timbers in his stride,
And the man from Snowy River never shifted in his seat —
It was grand to see that mountain horseman ride.
Through the stringy barks and saplings, on the rough and broken ground,
Down the hillside at a racing pace he went;
And he never drew the bridle till he landed safe and sound,
At the bottom of that terrible descent.

He was right among the horses as they climbed the farther hill
And the watchers on the mountain standing mute,
Saw him ply the stockwhip fiercely; he was right among them still,
As he raced across the clearing in pursuit.
Then they lost him for a moment, where two mountain gullies met

In the ranges - but a final glimpse reveals
On a dim and distant hillside the wild horses racing yet,
With the man from Snowy River at their heels.

And he ran them single-handed till their sides were white with foam.
He followed like a bloodhound on their track,
Till they halted cowed and beaten, then he turned their heads for home,
And alone and unassisted brought them back.
But his hardy mountain pony he could scarcely raise a trot,
He was blood from hip to shoulder from the spur;
But his pluck was still undaunted, and his courage fiery hot,
For never yet was mountain horse a cur.

And down by Kosciusko, where the pine-clad ridges raise
Their torn and rugged battlements on high,
Where the air is clear as crystal, and the white stars fairly blaze
At midnight in the cold and frosty sky,
And where around the Overflow the reed -beds sweep and sway
To the breezes, and the rolling plains are wide,
The man from Snowy River is a household word today,
And the stockmen tell the story of his ride.

A BUSH CHRISTENING

On the outer Barcoo where the churches are few,
    And men of religion are scanty,
On a road never cross'd 'cept by folk that are lost,
    One Michael Magee had a shanty.
Now this Mike was the dad of a ten year old lad,
    Plump, healthy, and stoutly conditioned;
He was strong as the best, but poor Mike had no rest
    For the youngster had never been christened.

And his wife used to cry, 'If the darlin' should die
    Saint Peter would not recognise him.'
But by luck he survived till a preacher arrived,
    Who agreed straightaway to baptise him.

Now the artful young rogue, while they held their collogue,
    With his ear to the keyhole was listenin',
And he muttered in fright, while his features turned white,
    'What the divil and all is this christenin'?'

He was none of your dolts, he had seen them brand colts,
    And it seemed to his small understanding,
If the man in the frock made him one of the flock,
    It must mean something very like branding.

So away with a rush he set off for the bush,
    While the tears in his eyelids they glistened —
''Tis outrageous,' says he, 'to brand youngsters like me,
    I'll be dashed if I'll stop to be christened!'

Like a young native dog he ran into a log,
    And his father with language uncivil,

Never heeding the 'praste' cried aloud in his haste,
'Come out and be christened, you divil!'

But he lay there as snug as a bug in a rug,
And his parents in vain might reprove him,
Till his reverence spoke (he was fond of a joke)
'I've a notion,' says he, 'that'll move him.'

'Poke a stick up the log, give the spalpeen a prog;
Poke him aisy — don't hurt him or maim him,
'Tis not long that he'll stand, I've the water at hand,
As he rushes out this end I'll name him.

'Here he comes, and for shame! ye've forgotten the name —
Is it Patsy or Michael or Dinnis?'
Here the youngster ran out, and the priest gave a shout —
'Take your chance, anyhow, wid 'Maginnis'!'

As the howling young cub ran away to the scrub
Where he knew that pursuit would be risky,
The priest, as he fled, flung a flask at his head
That was labelled 'MAGINNIS'S WHISKY'!

And Maginnis Magee has been made a J.P.,
And the one thing he hates more than sin is
To be asked by the folk, who have heard of the joke,
How he came to be christened 'Maginnis'!

THE MAN FROM IRONBARK

It was the man from Ironbark who struck the Sydney town,
He wandered over street and park, he wandered up and down.
He loitered here he loitered there, till he was like to drop,
Until at last in sheer despair he sought a barber's shop.
"Ere! shave my beard and whiskers off, I'll be a man of mark,
I'll go and do the Sydney toff up home in Ironbark."
The barber man was small and flash, as barbers mostly are,
He wore a strike-your-fancy sash he smoked a huge cigar;
He was a humorist of note and keen at repartee,
He laid the odds and kept a "tote", whatever that may be,
And when he saw our friend arrive, he whispered, "Here's a lark!
Just watch me catch him all alive, this man from Ironbark."

There were some gilded youths that sat along the barber's wall.
Their eyes were dull, their heads were flat, they had no brains at all;
To them the barber passed the wink his dexter eyelid shut,
"I'll make this bloomin' yokel think his bloomin' throat is cut."
And as he soaped and rubbed it in he made a rude remark:
"I s'pose the flats is pretty green up there in Ironbark."

A grunt was all reply he got; he shaved the bushman's chin,
Then made the water boiling hot and dipped the razor in.
He raised his hand, his brow grew black, he paused awhile to gloat,
Then slashed the red-hot razor-back across his victim's throat;
Upon the newly-shaven skin it made a livid mark
No doubt, it fairly took him in — the man from Ironbark.

He fetched a wild up-country yell might wake the dead to hear,
And though his throat, he knew full well, was cut from ear to ear,
He struggled gamely to his feet, and faced the murd'rous foe:
"You've done for me! you dog, I'm beat! One hit before I go!

I only wish I had a knife, you blessed murdering shark!
But you'll remember all your life the man from Ironbark."

He lifted up his hairy paw, with one tremendous clout
He landed on the barber's jaw, and knocked the barber out.
He set to work with nail and tooth, he made the place a wreck;
He grabbed the nearest gilded youth, and tried to break his neck.
And all the while his throat he held to save his vital spark,
And "Murder! Bloody murder!" yelled the man from Ironbark.

A peeler man who heard the din came in to see the show;
He tried to run the bushman in, but he refused to go.
And when at last the barber spoke, and said "'Twas all in fun'
T'was just a little harmless joke, a trifle overdone."
"A joke!" he cried, "By George, that's fine; a lively sort of lark;
I'd like to catch that murdering swine some night in Ironbark."

And now while round the shearing floor the list'ning shearers gape,
He tells the story o'er and o'er, and brags of his escape.
"Them barber chaps what keeps a tote, By George, I've had enough,
One tried to cut my bloomin' throat, but thank the Lord it's tough."
And whether he's believed or no, there's one thing to remark,
That flowing beards are all the go way up in Ironbark.

MULGA BILL'S BICYCLE

'Twas Mulga Bill, from Eaglehawk, that caught the cycling craze;
He turned away the good old horse that served him many days;
He dressed himself in cycling clothes, resplendent to be seen;
He hurried off to town and bought a shining new machine;
And as he wheeled it through the door, with air of lordly pride,
The grinning shop assistant said, "Excuse me, can you ride?"
"See here, young man," said Mulga Bill, "from Walgett to the sea,
From Conroy's Gap to Castlereagh, there's none can ride like me.
I'm good all round at everything, as everybody knows,
Although I'm not the one to talk - I hate a man that blows.
But riding is my special gift, my chiefest, sole delight;
Just ask a wild duck can it swim, a wildcat can it fight.
There's nothing clothed in hair or hide, or built of flesh or steel,
There's nothing walks or jumps, or runs, on axle, hoof, or wheel,
But what I'll sit, while hide will hold and girths and straps are tight:
I'll ride this here two-wheeled concern right straight away at sight."

'Twas Mulga Bill, from Eaglehawk, that sought his own abode,
That perched above the Dead Man's Creek, beside the mountain road.
He turned the cycle down the hill and mounted for the fray,
But ere he'd gone a dozen yards it bolted clean away.
It left the track, and through the trees, just like a silver streak,
It whistled down the awful slope towards the Dead Man's Creek.

It shaved a stump by half an inch, it dodged a big white-box:
The very wallaroos in fright went scrambling up the rocks,
The wombats hiding in their caves dug deeper underground,
As Mulga Bill, as white as chalk, sat tight to every bound.
It struck a stone and gave a spring that cleared a fallen tree,
It raced beside a precipice as close as close could be;
And then as Mulga Bill let out one last despairing shriek

It made a leap of twenty feet into the Dead Man's Creek.

'Twas Mulga Bill from Eaglehawk, that slowly swam ashore:
He said, "I've had some narrer shaves and lively rides before;
I've rode a wild bull round a yard to win a five-pound bet,
But this was the most awful ride that I've encountered yet.
I'll give that two-wheeled outlaw best; It's shaken all my nerve
To feel it whistle through the air and plunge and buck and swerve.
It's safe at rest in Dead Man's Creek, we'll leave it lying still;
A horse's back is good enough henceforth for Mulga Bill."

Clancy Of The Overflow

I had written him a letter which I had, for want of better
Knowledge, sent to where I met him down the Lachlan, years ago,
He was shearing when I knew him, so I sent the letter to him,
Just "on spec", addressed as follows, "Clancy, of The Overflow".

And an answer came directed in a writing unexpected,
(And I think the same was written with a thumb-nail dipped in tar)
Twas his shearing mate who wrote it, and verbatim I will quote it:
"Clancy's gone to Queensland droving, and we don't know where he are."

In my wild erratic fancy visions come to me of Clancy
Gone a-droving "down the Cooper" where the Western drovers go;
As the stock are slowly stringing, Clancy rides behind them singing,
For the drover's life has pleasures that the townsfolk never know.

And the bush hath friends to meet him, and their kindly voices greet him
In the murmur of the breezes and the river on its bars,
And he sees the vision splendid of the sunlit plains extended,
And at night the wond'rous glory of the everlasting stars.

I am sitting in my dingy little office, where a stingy
Ray of sunlight struggles feebly down between the houses tall,
And the foetid air and gritty of the dusty, dirty city
Through the open window floating, spreads its foulness over all

And in place of lowing cattle, I can hear the fiendish rattle
Of the tramways and the buses making hurry down the street,
And the language uninviting of the gutter children fighting,
Comes fitfully and faintly through the ceaseless tramp of feet.

And the hurrying people daunt me, and their pallid faces haunt me
As they shoulder one another in their rush and nervous haste,
With their eager eyes and greedy, and their stunted forms and weedy,
For townsfolk have no time to grow, they have no time to waste.

And I somehow rather fancy that I'd like to change with Clancy,
Like to take a turn at droving where the seasons come and go,
While he faced the round eternal of the cash-book and the journal —
But I doubt he'd suit the office, Clancy, of "The Overflow".

IN DEFENCE OF THE BUSH

So you're back from up the country, Mister Lawson, where you went,
And you're cursing all the business in a bitter discontent;
Well, we grieve to disappoint you, and it makes us sad to hear
That it wasn't cool and shady — and there wasn't whips of beer,
And the looney bullock snorted when you first came into view —
Well, you know it's not so often that he sees a swell like you;
And the roads were hot and dusty, and the plains were burnt and brown,
And no doubt you're better suited drinking lemon-squash in town.
Yet, perchance, if you should journey down the very track you went
In a month or two at furthest, you would wonder what it meant;
Where the sunbaked earth was gasping like a creature in itts pain
You would find the grasses waving like a field of summer grain,
And the miles of thirsty gutters, blocked with sand and choked with mud,
You would find them mighty rivers with a turbid, sweeping flood.
For the rain and drought and sunshine make no changes in the street,
In the sullen line of buildings and the ceaseless tramp of feet;
But the bush has moods and changes, as the seasons rise and fall,
And the men who know the bush-land — they are loyal through it all.

But you found the bush was dismal and a land of no delight —
Did you chance to hear a chorus in the shearers' huts at night?
Did they "rise up William Riley" by the camp-fire's cheery blaze?
Did they rise him as we rose him in the good old droving days?
And the women of the homesteads and the men you chanced to meet —
Were their faces sour and saddened like the "faces in the street"?
And the "shy selector children" — were they better now or worse
Than the little city urchins who would greet you with a curse?
Is not such a life much better than the squalid street and square
Where the fallen women flaunt it in the fierce electric glare,
Wher the sempstress plies her needle till her eyes are sore and red
In a filthy, dirty attic toiling on for daily bread?

Did you hear no sweeter voices in the music of the bush
Than the roar of trams and buses, and the war-whoop of "the push"?
Did the magpies rouse your slumbers with their carol sweet and strange?
Did you hear the silver chiming of the bell-birds on the range?
But, perchance, the wild birds' music by your senses was despised,
For you say you'll stay in townships till the bush is civilized.
Would you make it a tea-garden, and on Sundays have a band
Where the "blokes" might take their "donahs", with a "public" close at hand?
You had better stick to Sydney and make merry with the "push",
For the bush will never suit you, and you'll never suit the bush.

'We're All Australians Now'

Australia takes her pen in hand
To write a line to you,
To let you fellows understand
How proud we are of you.

From shearing shed and cattle run,
From Broome to Hobson's Bay,
Each native-born Australian son
Stands straighter up today.

The man who used to "hump his drum",
On far-out Queensland runs
Is fighting side by side with some
Tasmanian farmer's sons.

The fisher-boys dropped sail and oar
To grimly stand the test,
Along that storm-swept Turkish shore,
With miners from the west.

The old state jealousies of yore
Are dead as Pharaoh's sow,
We're not State children any more —
We're all Australians now!

Our six-starred flag that used to fly
Half-shyly to the breeze,
Unknown where older nations ply
Their trade on foreign seas,

Flies out to meet the morning blue
With Vict'ry at the prow;
For that's the flag the Sydney flew,
The wide seas know it now!

The mettle that a race can show
Is proved with shot and steel,
And now we know what nations know
And feel what nations feel.

The honoured graves beneath the crest
Of Gaba Tepe hill
May hold our bravest and our best,
But we have brave men still.

With all our petty quarrels done,
Dissensions overthrown,
We have, through what you boys have done,
A history of our own.

Our old world diff'rences are dead,
Like weeds beneath the plough,

For English, Scotch, and Irish-bred,
They're all Australians now!

So now we'll toast the Third Brigade
That led Australia's van,
For never shall their glory fade
In minds Australian.

Fight on, fight on, unflinchingly,
Till right and justice reign.
Fight on, fight on, till Victory
Shall send you home again.

And with Australia's flag shall fly
A spray of wattle-bough
To symbolise our unity —
We're all Australians now.

AS LONG AS YOUR EYES ARE BLUE

Wilt thou love me, sweet, when my hair is grey
And my cheeks shall have lost their hue?
When the charms of youth shall have passed away,
Will your love as of old prove true?

For the looks may change, and the heart may range,
And the love be no longer fond;
Wilt thou love with truth in the years of youth
And away to the years beyond?

Oh, I love you, sweet, for your locks of brown
And the blush on your cheek that lies —
But I love you most for the kindly heart
That I see in your sweet blue eyes.

For the eyes are signs of the soul within,
Of the heart that is leal and true,
And mine own sweetheart, I shall love you still,
Just as long as your eyes are blue.

For the locks may bleach, and the cheeks of peach
May be reft of their golden hue;
But mine own sweetheart, I shall love you still,
Just as long as your eyes are blue.

HENRY LAWSON

Henry Archibald Hertzberg Lawson was an Australian writer and bush poet. Along with his contemporary Banjo Paterson, Lawson is among the best-known Australian poets and fiction writers of the colonial period and is often called Australia's "greatest short story writer." In 1884 he moved to Sydney, where the Bulletin published his first stories and verses (1887–88). During those years, he worked for several newspapers and spent much time wandering. Out of these experiences came material for his vivid, realistic writing, which, by its often pessimistic blend of pathos and irony, captured some of the spirits of Australian working life. Many of his works helped popularise the Australian vernacular in fiction.

UP THE COUNTRY

I am back from up the country — very sorry that I went —
Seeking for the Southern poets' land whereon to pitch my tent;
I have lost a lot of idols, which were broken on the track,
Burnt a lot of fancy verses, and I'm glad that I am back.
Further out may be the pleasant scenes of which our poets boast,
But I think the country's rather more inviting round the coast.
Anyway, I'll stay at present at a boarding-house in town,
Drinking beer and lemon-squashes, taking baths and cooling down.

`Sunny plains'! Great Scott! — those burning
wastes of barren soil and sand
With their everlasting fences stretching out across the land!
Desolation where the crow is! Desert where the eagle flies,
Paddocks where the luny bullock starts and stares with reddened eyes;
Where, in clouds of dust enveloped, roasted bullock-drivers creep
Slowly past the sun-dried shepherd dragged behind his crawling sheep.
Stunted peak of granite gleaming, glaring like a molten mass
Turned from some infernal furnace on a plain devoid of grass.

Miles and miles of thirsty gutters — strings of muddy water-holes
In the place of `shining rivers' — `walled by cliffs and forest boles.'
Barren ridges, gullies, ridges! where the ever-madd'ning flies —
Fiercer than the plagues of Egypt — swarm about your blighted eyes!
Bush! where there is no horizon! where the buried bushman sees
Nothing — Nothing! but the sameness of the ragged, stunted trees!
Lonely hut where drought's eternal, suffocating atmosphere
Where the God-forgotten hatter dreams of city life and beer.

Treacherous tracks that trap the stranger,
endless roads that gleam and glare,
Dark and evil-looking gullies, hiding secrets here and there!

Dull dumb flats and stony rises, where the toiling bullocks bake,
And the sinister `gohanna', and the lizard, and the snake.
Land of day and night — no morning freshness, and no afternoon,
When the great white sun in rising bringeth summer heat in June.
Dismal country for the exile, when the shades begin to fall
From the sad heart-breaking sunset, to the new-chum worst of all.

Dreary land in rainy weather, with the endless clouds that drift
O'er the bushman like a blanket that the Lord will never lift —
Dismal land when it is raining — growl of floods, and, oh! the woosh
Of the rain and wind together on the dark bed of the bush —
Ghastly fires in lonely humpies where the granite rocks are piled
In the rain-swept wildernesses that are wildest of the wild.

Land where gaunt and haggard women live alone and work like men,
Till their husbands, gone a-droving, will return to them again:
Homes of men! if home had ever such a God-forgotten place,
Where the wild selector's children fly before a stranger's face.
Home of tragedy applauded by the dingoes' dismal yell,
Heaven of the shanty-keeper — fitting fiend for such a hell —
And the wallaroos and wombats, and, of course, the curlew's call —
And the lone sundowner tramping ever onward through it all!

I am back from up the country, up the country where I went
Seeking for the Southern poets' land whereon to pitch my tent;
I have shattered many idols out along the dusty track,
Burnt a lot of fancy verses — and I'm glad that I am back.
I believe the Southern poets' dream will not be realised
Till the plains are irrigated and the land is humanised.
I intend to stay at present, as I said before, in town
Drinking beer and lemon-squashes, taking baths and cooling down.

ANDY'S GONE WITH CATTLE

Our Andy's gone to battle now
'Gainst Drought, the red marauder;
Our Andy's gone with cattle now
Across the Queensland border.

He's left us in dejection now;
Our hearts with him are roving.
It's dull on this selection now,
Since Andy went a-droving.

Who now shall wear the cheerful face
In times when things are slackest?
And who shall whistle round the place
When Fortune frowns her blackest?

Oh, who shall cheek the squatter now
When he comes round us snarling?
His tongue is growing hotter now
Since Andy cross'd the Darling.

The gates are out of order now,
In storms the 'riders' rattle;
For far across the border now
Our Andy's gone with cattle.

Poor Aunty's looking thin and white;
And Uncle's cross with worry;
And poor old Blucher howls all night
Since Andy left Macquarie.

Oh, may the showers in torrents fall,

And all the tanks run over;
And may the grass grow green and tall
In pathways of the drover;

And may good angels send the rain
On desert stretches sandy;
And when the summer comes again
God grant 'twill bring us Andy.

IN THE DAY'S WHEN WE ARE DEAD

Listen! The end draws nearer,
Nearer the morning—or night—
And I see with a vision clearer
That the beginning was right!
These shall be words to remember
When all has been done and said,
And my fame is a dying ember
In the days when I am dead.
Listen! We wrote in sorrow,
And we wrote by candle light;
We took no heed of the morrow,
And I think that we were right—
(To-morrow, but not the day after,
And I think that we were right).

We wrote of a world that was human
And we wrote of blood that was red,
For a child, or a man, or a woman—
Remember when we are dead.

Listen! We wrote not for money,
And listen! We wrote not for fame—
We wrote for the milk and the honey
Of Kindness, and not for a name.

We paused not, nor faltered for any,
Though many fell back where we led;
We wrote of the few for the many—
Remember when we are dead.

We suffered as few men suffer,

Yet laughed as few men laugh;
We grin as the road grows rougher,
And a bitterer cup we quaff.

We lived for Right and for Laughter,
And we fought for a Nation ahead—
Remember it, friends, hereafter,
In the years when I am dead—
For to-morrow and not the day after,
For ourselves, and a Nation ahead.

FREEDOM ON THE WALLABY

Australia's a big country
An' Freedom's humping bluey,
An' Freedom's on the wallaby
Oh! don't you hear 'er cooey?
She's just begun to boomerang,
She'll knock the tyrants silly,
She's goin' to light another fire
And boil another billy.

Our fathers toiled for bitter bread
While loafers thrived beside 'em,
But food to eat and clothes to wear,
Their native land denied 'em.
An' so they left their native land
In spite of their devotion,
An' so they came, or if they stole,
Were sent across the ocean.

Then Freedom couldn't stand the glare
O' Royalty's regalia,
She left the loafers where they were,
An' came out to Australia.
But now across the mighty main
The chains have come ter bind her –
She little thought to see again
The wrongs she left behind her.

Our parents toil'd to make a home –
Hard grubbin 'twas an' clearin' –
They wasn't crowded much with lords
When they was pioneering.

But now that we have made the land
A garden full of promise,
Old Greed must crook 'is dirty hand
And come ter take it from us.

So we must fly a rebel flag,
As others did before us,
And we must sing a rebel song
And join in rebel chorus.
We'll make the tyrants feel the sting
O' those that they would throttle;
They needn't say the fault is ours
If blood should stain the wattle!

THE CITY BUSHMAN

It was pleasant up the country, Mr. Banjo, where you went,
For you sought the greener patches and you travelled like a gent;
And you curse the trams and buses and the turmoil and the push,
Though you know the squalid city needn't keep you from the bush;
But we lately heard you singing of the `plains where shade is not',
And you mentioned it was dusty -- `all was dry and all was hot'.

True, the bush `hath moods and changes' -- and the bushman hath 'em, too,
For he's not a poet's dummy -- he's a man, the same as you;
But his back is growing rounder -- slaving for the absentee --
And his toiling wife is thinner than a country wife should be.
For we noticed that the faces of the folks we chanced to meet
Should have made a greater contrast to the faces in the street;
And, in short, we think the bushman's being driven to the wall,
And it's doubtful if his spirit will be `loyal thro' it all'.

Though the bush has been romantic and it's nice to sing about,
There's a lot of patriotism that the land could do without --
Sort of BRITISH WORKMAN nonsense that shall perish in the scorn
Of the drover who is driven and the shearer who is shorn,
Of the struggling western farmers who have little time for rest,
And are ruined on selections in the sheep-infested West;
Droving songs are very pretty, but they merit little thanks
From the people of a country in possession of the Banks.

And the `rise and fall of seasons' suits the rise and fall of rhyme,
But we know that western seasons do not run on schedule time;
For the drought will go on drying while there's anything to dry,
Then it rains until you'd fancy it would bleach the sunny sky --
Then it pelters out of reason, for the downpour day and night
Nearly sweeps the population to the Great Australian Bight.

It is up in Northern Queensland that the seasons do their best,
But it's doubtful if you ever saw a season in the West;
There are years without an autumn or a winter or a spring,
There are broiling Junes, and summers when it rains like anything.

In the bush my ears were opened to the singing of the bird,
But the `carol of the magpie' was a thing I never heard.
Once the beggar roused my slumbers in a shanty, it is true,
But I only heard him asking, `Who the blanky blank are you?'
And the bell-bird in the ranges -- but his `silver chime' is harsh
When it's heard beside the solo of the curlew in the marsh.

Yes, I heard the shearers singing `William Riley', out of tune,
Saw 'em fighting round a shanty on a Sunday afternoon,
But the bushman isn't always `trapping brumbies in the night',
Nor is he for ever riding when `the morn is fresh and bright',
And he isn't always singing in the humpies on the run --
And the camp-fire's `cheery blazes' are a trifle overdone;
We have grumbled with the bushmen round the fire on rainy days,
When the smoke would blind a bullock and there wasn't any blaze,
Save the blazes of our language, for we cursed the fire in turn
Till the atmosphere was heated and the wood began to burn.
Then we had to wring our blueys which were rotting in the swags,
And we saw the sugar leaking through the bottoms of the bags,
And we couldn't raise a chorus, for the toothache and the cramp,
While we spent the hours of darkness draining puddles round the camp.

Would you like to change with Clancy -- go a-droving? tell us true,
For we rather think that Clancy would be glad to change with you,
And be something in the city; but 'twould give your muse a shock
To be losing time and money through the foot-rot in the flock,
And you wouldn't mind the beauties underneath the starry dome

If you had a wife and children and a lot of bills at home.

Did you ever guard the cattle when the night was inky-black,
And it rained, and icy water trickled gently down your back
Till your saddle-weary backbone fell a-aching to the roots
And you almost felt the croaking of the bull-frog in your boots --
Sit and shiver in the saddle, curse the restless stock and cough
Till a squatter's irate dummy cantered up to warn you off?
Did you fight the drought and pleuro when the `seasons' were asleep,
Felling sheoaks all the morning for a flock of starving sheep,
Drinking mud instead of water -- climbing trees and lopping boughs
For the broken-hearted bullocks and the dry and dusty cows?

Do you think the bush was better in the `good old droving days',
When the squatter ruled supremely as the king of western ways,
When you got a slip of paper for the little you could earn,
But were forced to take provisions from the station in return --
When you couldn't keep a chicken at your humpy on the run,
For the squatter wouldn't let you -- and your work was never done;
When you had to leave the missus in a lonely hut forlorn
While you `rose up Willy Riley' -- in the days ere you were born?

Ah! we read about the drovers and the shearers and the like
Till we wonder why such happy and romantic fellows strike.
Don't you fancy that the poets ought to give the bush a rest
Ere they raise a just rebellion in the over-written West?
Where the simple-minded bushman gets a meal and bed and rum
Just by riding round reporting phantom flocks that never come;
Where the scalper -- never troubled by the `war-whoop of the push' --
Has a quiet little billet -- breeding rabbits in the bush;
Where the idle shanty-keeper never fails to make a draw,
And the dummy gets his tucker through provisions in the law;

Where the labour-agitator -- when the shearers rise in might --
Makes his money sacrificing all his substance for The Right;
Where the squatter makes his fortune, and `the seasons rise and fall',
And the poor and honest bushman has to suffer for it all;
Where the drovers and the shearers and the bushmen and the rest
Never reach the Eldorado of the poets of the West.

And you think the bush is purer and that life is better there,
But it doesn't seem to pay you like the `squalid street and square'.
Pray inform us, City Bushman, where you read, in prose or verse,
Of the awful `city urchin who would greet you with a curse'.
There are golden hearts in gutters, though their owners lack the fat,
And we'll back a teamster's offspring to outswear a city brat.
Do you think we're never jolly where the trams and buses rage?
Did you hear the gods in chorus when `Ri-tooral' held the stage?
Did you catch a ring of sorrow in the city urchin's voice
When he yelled for Billy Elton, when he thumped the floor for Royce?
Do the bushmen, down on pleasure, miss the everlasting stars
When they drink and flirt and so on in the glow of private bars?

You've a down on `trams and buses', or the `roar' of 'em, you said,
And the `filthy, dirty attic', where you never toiled for bread.
(And about that self-same attic -- Lord! wherever have you been?
For the struggling needlewoman mostly keeps her attic clean.)
But you'll find it very jolly with the cuff-and-collar push,
And the city seems to suit you, while you rave about the bush.

. . . . .

You'll admit that Up-the Country, more especially in drought,
Isn't quite the Eldorado that the poets rave about,
Yet at times we long to gallop where the reckless bushman rides
In the wake of startled brumbies that are flying for their hides;
Long to feel the saddle tremble once again between our knees

And to hear the stockwhips rattle just like rifles in the trees!
Long to feel the bridle-leather tugging strongly in the hand
And to feel once more a little like a native of the land.
And the ring of bitter feeling in the jingling of our rhymes
Isn't suited to the country nor the spirit of the times.
Let us go together droving, and returning, if we live,
Try to understand each other while we reckon up the div.

THE SONG OF AUSTRALIA

The centuries found me to nations unknown –
My people have crowned me and made me a throne;
My royal regalia is love, truth, and light –
A girl called Australia – I've come to my right.

Though no fields of conquest grew red at my birth,
My dead were the noblest and bravest on earth;
Their strong sons are worthy to stand with the best –
My brave Overlanders ride west of the west.

My cities are seeking the clean and the right;
My Statesmen are speaking in London to-night;
The voice of my Bushmen is heard oversea;
My army and navy are coming to me.

By all my grim headlands my flag is unfurled,
My artists and singers are charming the world;
The White world shall know its young outpost with pride;
The fame of my poets goes ever more wide.

By old tow'r and steeple of nation grown grey
The name of my people is spreading to-day;
Through all the old nations my learners go forth;
My youthful inventors are startling the north.

In spite of all Asia, and safe from her yet,
Through wide Australasia my standards I'll set;
A grand world and bright world to rise in an hour –
The Wings of the White world, the Balance of Power.

Through storm, or serenely – whate'er I go through –
God grant I be queenly! God grant I be true!
To suffer in silence, and strike at a sign,
Till all the fair islands of these seas are mine.

THE MAN FROM WATERLOO
(WITH KIND REGARDS TO BANJO)

It was the Man from Waterloo,
When work in town was slack,
Who took the track as bushmen do,
And humped his swag out back.
He tramped for months without a bob,
For most the sheds were full,
Until at last he got a job
At picking up the wool.
He found the work was rather rough,
But swore to see it through,
For he was made of sterling stuff—
The Man from Waterloo.
The first remark was like a stab
That fell his ear upon,
'Twas—'There's another something scab
'The boss has taken on!'
They couldn't let the towny be—
They sneered like anything;
They'd mock him when he'd sound the 'g'
In words that end in 'ing.'

There came a man from Ironbark,
And at the shed he shore;
He scoffed his victuals like a shark,
And like a fiend he swore.
He'd shorn his flowing beard that day—
He found it hard to reap—
Because 'twas hot and in the way
While he was shearing sheep.

His loaded fork in grimy holt
Was poised, his jaws moved fast,
Impatient till his throat could bolt
The mouthful taken last.
He couldn't stand a something toff;
Much less a jackaroo;
And swore to take the trimmings off
The Man from Waterloo.

The towny saw he must be up
Or else be underneath,
And so one day, before them all,
He dared to clean his teeth.
The men came running from the shed,
And shouted, 'Here's a lark!'
'It's gone to clean its tooties!' said
The man from Ironbark.
His feeble joke was much enjoyed;
He sneered as bullies do,
And with a scrubbing-brush he guyed
The Man from Waterloo.

The Jackaroo made no remark
But peeled and waded in,
And soon the Man from Ironbark
Had three teeth less to grin!
And when they knew that he could fight
They swore to see him through,
Because they saw that he was right—
The Man from Waterloo.

Now in a shop in Sydney, near

The Bottle on the Shelf,
The tale is told—with trimmings—by
The Jackaroo himself.
'They made my life a hell,' he said;
'They wouldn't let me be;
They set the bully of the shed
'To take it out of me.

'The dirt was on him like a sheath,
'He seldom washed his phiz;
'He sneered because I cleaned my teeth—
'I guess I dusted his!
'I treated them as they deserved—
'I signed on one or two!
'They won't forget me soon,' observed
The Man from Waterloo.

DOROTHEA MACKELLER

Isobel Marion Dorothea Mackellar, OBE, was an Australian poet and fiction writer. Her poem 'My Country' is widely known in Australia. Written after spending time traveling in Europe, "My Country" describes the land of Australia in lyric detail, especially its second stanza: "I love a sunburnt country/A land of sweeping plains, / Of ragged mountain ranges, /Of droughts and flooding rains." Mackellar began writing early, and her first poems were published at the beginning of the 20th century. In addition to poetry, Mackellar also wrote novels. She published Outlaw's Luck in 1913 and wrote two books in collaboration with Ruth Bedford, The Little Blue Devil (1912) and Two's Company (1914). Her work, including the poems "Dawn" and "Burning Off," was often influenced by her time spent at her family's country homes near Gunnedah in New South Wales.

MY COUNTRY (1908)

The love of field and coppice
Of green and shaded lanes,
Of ordered woods and gardens
Is running in your veins.
Strong love of grey-blue distance,
Brown streams and soft, dim skies
I know, but cannot share it,
My love is otherwise.

I love a sunburnt country,
A land of sweeping plains,
Of ragged mountain ranges,
Of droughts and flooding rains.
I love her far horizons,
I love her jewel-sea,
Her beauty and her terror
The wide brown land for me!

The stark white ring-barked forests,
All tragic to the moon,
The sapphire-misted mountains,
The hot gold hush of noon,
Green tangle of the brushes
Where lithe lianas coil,
And orchids deck the tree-tops,
And ferns the warm dark soil.

Core of my heart, my country!
Her pitiless blue sky,
When, sick at heart, around us
We see the cattle die

But then the grey clouds gather,
And we can bless again
The drumming of an army,
The steady soaking rain.

Core of my heart, my country!
Land of the rainbow gold,
For flood and fire and famine
She pays us back threefold.
Over the thirsty paddocks,
Watch, after many days,
The filmy veil of greenness
That thickens as we gaze ...

An opal-hearted country,
A wilful, lavish land
All you who have not loved her,
You will not understand
though Earth holds many splendours,
Wherever I may die,
I know to what brown country
My homing thoughts will fly.

THE COLOURS OF LIGHT (1914)

This is not easy to understand
For you that come from a distant land
Where all thecolours are low in pitch -
Deep purples, emeralds deep and rich,
Where autumn's flaming and summer's green -
Here is a beauty you have not seen.

All is pitched in a higher key,
Lilac, topaz, and ivory,
Palest jade-green and pale clear blue
Like aquamarines that the sun shines through,
Golds and silvers, we have at will -
Silver and gold on each plain and hill,
Silver-green of the myall leaves,
Tawny gold of the garnered sheaves,
Silver rivers that silent slide,
Golden sands by the water-side,

Golden wattle, and golden broom,
Silver stars of the rosewood bloom;
Amber sunshine, and smoke-blue shade:
Opal colours that glow and fade;
On the gold of the upland grass
Blue cloud-shadows that swiftly pass;
Wood-smoke blown in an azure mist;
Hills of tenuous amethyst. . .

Oft the colours are pitched so high
The deepest note is the cobalt sky;
We have to wait till the sunset comes
For shades that feel like the beat of drums -

Or like organ notes in their rise and fall -
Purple and orange and cardinal,
Or the peacock-green that turns soft and slow
To peacock-blue as the great stars show . . .

Sugar-gum boles flushed to peach-blow pink;
Blue-gums, tall at the clearing's brink;
Ivory pillars, their smooth fine slope
Dappled with delicate heliotrope;
Grey of the twisted mulga-roots;
Golden-bronze of the budding shoots;
Tints of the lichens that cling and spread,
Nile-green, primrose, and palest red . . .

Sheen of the bronze-wing; blue of the crane;
Fawn and pearl of the lyrebird's train;
Cream of the plover; grey of the dove -
These are the hues of the land I love.

BURNING OFF (1911)

They're burning off at the Rampadells,
The tawny flames uprise,
With greedy licking around the trees;
The fierce breath sears our eyes.

From cores already grown furnace-hot -
The logs are well alight!
We fling more wood where the flameless heart
Is throbbing red and white.

The fire bites deep in that beating heart,
The creamy smoke-wreaths ooze
From cracks and knot-holes along the trunk
To melt in greys and blues.

The young horned moon has gone from the sky,
And night has settled down;
A red glare shows from the Rampadells,
Grim as a burning town.

Full seven fathoms above the rest
A tree stands, great and old,
A red-hot column whence fly the sparks,
One ceaseless shower of gold.

All hail the king of the fire before
He sway and crack and crash
To earth - for surely tomorrow's sun
Will see him white fine ash.

The king in his robe of falling stars,
No trace shall leave behind,
And where he stood with his silent court,
The wheat shall bow to the wind.

FIRE (1914)

This life that we call our own
Is neither strong nor free;
A flame in the wind of death,
It trembles ceaselessly.

And this all we can do
To use our little light
Before, in the piercing wind,
It flickers into night:

To yield the heat of the flame,
To grudge not, but to give
Whatever we have of strength,
That one more flame may live.

COLOUR
(1914)

The lovely things that I have watched unthinking,
Unknowing, day by day,
That their soft dyes have steeped my soul in colour
That will not pass away -

Great saffron sunset clouds, and larkspur mountains,
And fenceless miles of plain,
And hillsides golden-green in that unearthly
Clear shining after rain;

And nights of blue and pearl, and long smooth beaches,
Yellow as sunburnt wheat,
Edged with a line of foam that creams and hisses,
Enticing weary feet.

And emeralds, and sunset-hearted opals,
And Asian marble, veined
With scarlet flame, and cool green jade, and moonstones
Misty and azure-stained;

And almond trees in bloom, and oleanders,
Or a wide purple sea,
Of plain-land gorgeous with a lovely poison,
The evil Darling pea.

If I am tired I call on these to help me
To dream -and dawn-lit skies,
Lemon and pink, or faintest, coolest lilac,
Float on my soothed eyes.

There is no night so black but you shine through it,
There is no morn so drear,
O Colour of the World, but I can find you,
Most tender, pure and clear.

Thanks be to God, Who gave this gift of colour,
Which who shall seek shall find;
Thanks be to God, Who gives me strength to hold it,
Though I were stricken blind.

AN OLD SONG

The almond bloom is overpast, the apple blossoms blow.
I never loved but one man, and I never told him so.

My flowers will never come to fruit, but I have kept my pride -
A little, cold, and lonely thing, and I have naught beside.

The spring-wind caught my flowering dreams, they lightly blew away.
I never had but one true love, and he died yesterday.

THE CLOSED DOOR

As we crossed Alcántara
With the Tagus falling,
I was 'ware there came a voice
At my shoulder calling.
As we climbed the steep red path—
Red as smouldering ember—
"You, you know this well," it said,
"Do you not remember?"

Up the narrow cobbled streets
Still it followed after,
Whispering deeds that we had shared
With a fierce low laughter.
"Here you stabbed him and he fell
With his sword a-clatter
Life for life—you paid your debt—
That was no great matter."

Through the Gate that Wamba built
Still the voice pursuing
Softly called, "We know it all,
All that you are doing.
Every stone you're treading now
You have known aforetime,
You have seen these grim red walls
In the stress of wartime.

"You remember? Down this lane
You would often swagger
With your comrades of the mask,
Cloak and sword and dagger.

At that window high she stood,
Some dear dead Dolores....
You've forgotten—and so soon?
—There are other stories...."

By the white Church of the Kings,
By the proud red towers,
Thronging round about me came
Ghosts of long-dead hours;
Ghosts of many a blazing June,
Many a keen December—
"Thus and thus and thus we did.
Do you not remember?"
Toledo, Spain.

THE WITCH-MAID

I wandered in the woodland a morning in the spring,
I found a glade I had not known, and saw an evil thing.

I heard a wood-dove calling, as one that loves and grieves,
The sun was shining silver on the small bright leaves,
O it was very beautiful, the glade that I had found!
I peeped between the slender stems, and there upon the ground
A man was lying dead, and from the spear-wound in his side
The sluggish blood had ceased to flow, and yet had hardly dried.

O the shining of the leaves,
The morning of the year!
O how could any die to-day, with life so young and dear?
My feet were tied with horror, I could not turn to run;
A light breeze tossed the branches, the shadow and the sun
Across the dead face shifted—it seemed to change and twitch—
When from the trees beyond me stepped a white young witch.

I prayed that I was hidden, she never turned her head,
But picked her footsteps daintily and stooped beside the dead;
She touched him with her hanging hair and stroked him with her hand,
Still gazing like a little child that does not understand,
For she had strayed from Elfland where death has never come,
She knew not why his side was torn nor why his mouth was dumb.

She sat her down beside him and joined her finger-tips
And smiled a strange and secret smile that curved her thin red lips;
She wore a veil of purple about her body sweet
And little silver sandals on her smooth pale feet;
Her black hair hung as straight as rain and touched the dead man's eyes,
He smiled at her in answer, a scornful smile and wise.

She played with him awhile as might a panther-kitten play,
Most horrible it was, and yet I could not look away—
I needs must watch her motions, her cruel, supple grace,
The delicate swift changes of her sharp-cut face;
Till suddenly she wearied, and rising from her knees
All in one lovely movement like a sapling in the breeze,
She gazed on him who would not play, with gathering surprise—
The man she did not understand, though she was very wise
She drew her veil around her, her whiteness showing through,
And gazed; and still unceasingly there came the wood-dove's coo.

O the stirring of the spring,
The calling of the dove!
Why does he lie so cold, so cold, when I am here to love?

Her long strange eyes were narrowed to threads of shining green,
She touched the broken spear-point the wound's red lips between,
She touched it with her careless foot, and yet he did not stir,
Dull fool that lay with open eyes and would not look at her!

She turned away in anger and raised her arms on high,
Her straight white arms that questioned the pure pale sky,
The thousand slender tree-stems soon hid the way she went
As they who hold a secret and therewith are content.
The dead man smiled in silence; a strange thought in me said,
If I had heard her speak at all then I too should be dead:
Her voice—what would her voice be?—and then I fled, afraid,
The spell was loosed that bound me to the evil glade.

O the flowers in the grass,
The wood-dove in the tree;
From magic and from sudden death, Good Lord deliver me!

PILGRIM SONG

My feet are grey with the roadside dust,
My hair is wet with the dew,
My heart is flagging with weariness
And faint with the want of you.
You are as young as the breaking buds,
You are as old as the sea;
My soul burns white in the flame of you—
Love, open your door to me!...
I sought my love in the noontide heat,
I sought in the bitter wind,
And found her house—and the doors were shut,
And the windows were barred and blind.

ADAM LINDSAY GORDON

Adam Lindsay Gordon was a British-Australian poet, horseman, police officer, and politician. He was the first Australian poet to gain considerable recognition overseas. According to his contemporary, writer Marcus Clarke, Gordon's work represented "the beginnings of a national school of Australian poetry." He was one of the first poets to write in a distinctly Australian idiom. Gordon's solid rhythms and homespun philosophy make his poetry memorable. His work was eventually widely accepted, and some of his lines have been adopted into the Australian vernacular. In the decades following Gordon's death, his work drew increasing praise from literary figures and the public. Especially in Melbourne, he was exalted as a genius and a national poet. Arthur Conan Doyle and Oscar Wilde counted among his admirers, hailing him as "one of the finest poetic singers the English race has ever known."

A SONG OF AUTUMN

'WHERE shall we go for our garlands glad
At the falling of the year,
When the burnt-up banks are yellow and sad,
When the boughs are yellow and sere?
Where are the old ones that once we had,
And when are the new ones near?
What shall we do for our garlands glad
At the falling of the year?'
'Child! can I tell where the garlands go?
Can I say where the lost leaves veer
On the brown-burnt banks, when the wild winds blow,
When they drift through the dead-wood drear?
Girl! when the garlands of next year glow,
You may gather again, my dear—
But I go where the last year's lost leaves go
At the falling of the year.'

THE SICK STOCKRIDER

Hold hard, Ned! Lift me down once more, and lay me in the shade.
  Old man, you've had your work cut out to guide
Both horses, and to hold me in the saddle when I swayed,
  All through the hot, slow, sleepy, silent ride.
The dawn at "Moorabinda" was a mist rack dull and dense,
  The sun-rise was a sullen, sluggish lamp;
I was dozing in the gateway at Arbuthnot's bound'ry fence,
  I was dreaming on the Limestone cattle camp.
We crossed the creek at Carricksford, and sharply through the haze,
  And suddenly the sun shot flaming forth;
To southward lay "Katawa", with the sand peaks all ablaze,
  And the flushed fields of Glen Lomond lay to north.
Now westward winds the bridle-path that leads to Lindisfarm,
  And yonder looms the double-headed Bluff;
From the far side of the first hill, when the skies are clear and calm,
  You can see Sylvester's woolshed fair enough.
Five miles we used to call it from our homestead to the place
  Where the big tree spans the roadway like an arch;
'Twas here we ran the dingo down that gave us such a chase
  Eight years ago — or was it nine? — last March.
'Twas merry in the glowing morn among the gleaming grass,
  To wander as we've wandered many a mile,
And blow the cool tobacco cloud, and watch the white wreaths pass,
  Sitting loosely in the saddle all the while.
'Twas merry 'mid the blackwoods, when we spied the station roofs,
  To wheel the wild scrub cattle at the yard,
With a running fire of stock whips and a fiery run of hoofs;
  Oh! the hardest day was never then too hard!
Aye! we had a glorious gallop after "Starlight" and his gang,
  When they bolted from Sylvester's on the flat;
How the sun-dried reed-beds crackled, how the flint-strewn ranges rang,

To the strokes of "Mountaineer" and "Acrobat".
Hard behind them in the timber, harder still across the heath,
Close beside them through the tea-tree scrub we dash'd;
And the golden-tinted fern leaves, how they rustled underneath;
And the honeysuckle osiers, how they crash'd!
We led the hunt throughout, Ned, on the chestnut and the grey,
And the troopers were three hundred yards behind,
While we emptied our six-shooters on the bushrangers at bay,
In the creek with stunted box-trees for a blind!
There you grappled with the leader, man to man, and horse to horse,
And you roll'd together when the chestnut rear'd;
He blazed away and missed you in that shallow water-course —
A narrow shave — his powder singed your beard!

In these hours when life is ebbing, how those days when life was young
Come back to us; how clearly I recall
Even the yarns Jack Hall invented, and the songs Jem Roper sung;
And where are now Jem Roper and Jack Hall?
Ay! nearly all our comrades of the old colonial school,
Our ancient boon companions, Ned, are gone;
Hard livers for the most part, somewhat reckless as a rule,
It seems that you and I are left alone.
There was Hughes, who got in trouble through that business with the cards,
It matters little what became of him;
But a steer ripp'd up Macpherson in the Cooraminta yards,
And Sullivan was drown'd at Sink-or-swim;
And Mostyn — poor Frank Mostyn — died at last, a fearful wreck,
In the "horrors" at the Upper Wandinong,
And Carisbrooke, the rider, at the Horsefall broke his neck;
Faith! the wonder was he saved his neck so long!

Ah! those days and nights we squandered at the Logans' in the glen —

The Logans, man and wife, have long been dead.
Elsie's tallest girl seems taller than your little Elsie then;
And Ethel is a woman grown and wed.

I've had my share of pastime, and I've done my share of toil,
And life is short — the longest life a span;
I care not now to tarry for the corn or for the oil,
Or for wine that maketh glad the heart of man.
For good undone, and gifts misspent, and resolutions vain,
'Tis somewhat late to trouble. This I know —
I should live the same life over, if I had to live again;
And the chances are I go where most men go.

The deep blue skies wax dusky, and the tall green trees grow dim,
The sward beneath me seems to heave and fall;
And sickly, smoky shadows through the sleepy sunlight swim,
And on the very sun's face weave their pall.
Let me slumber in the hollow where the wattle blossoms wave,
With never stone or rail to fence my bed;
Should the sturdy station children pull the bush-flowers on my grave,
I may chance to hear them romping overhead.

I don't suppose I shall though, for I feel like sleeping sound,
That sleep, they say, is doubtful. True; but yet
At least it makes no difference to the dead man underground
What the living men remember or forget.
Enigmas that perplex us in the world's unequal strife,
The future may ignore or may reveal;
Yet some, as weak as water, Ned, to make the best of life,
Have been to face the worst as true as steel.

THE SWIMMER

With short, sharp, violent lights made vivid,
To southward far as the sight can roam,
Only the swirl of the surges livid,
The seas that climb and the surfs that comb.
Only the crag and the cliff to nor'ward,
And the rocks receding, and reefs flung forward,
And waifs wreck'd seaward and wasted shoreward
On shallows sheeted with flaming foam.

A grim, grey coast and a seaboard ghastly,
And shores trod seldom by feet of men—
Where the batter'd hull and the broken mast lie,
They have lain embedded these long years ten.
Love! when we wander'd here together,
Hand in hand through the sparkling weather,
From the heights and hollows of fern and heather,
God surely loved us a little then.

The skies were fairer and shores were firmer—
The blue sea over the bright sand roll'd;
Babble and prattle, and ripple and murmur,
Sheen of silver and glamour of gold—
And the sunset bath'd in the gulf to lend her
A garland of pinks and of purples tender,
A tinge of the sun-god's rosy splendour,
A tithe of his glories manifold.

Man's works are graven, cunning, and skilful
On earth, where his tabernacles are;
But the sea is wanton, the sea is wilful,
And who shall mend her and who shall mar?

Shall we carve success or record disaster
On the bosom of her heaving alabaster?
Will her purple pulse beat fainter or faster
For fallen sparrow or fallen star?

I would that with sleepy, soft embraces
The sea would fold me—would find me rest,
In luminous shades of her secret places,
In depths where her marvels are manifest;
So the earth beneath her should not discover
My hidden couch—nor the heaven above her—
As a strong love shielding a weary lover,
I would have her shield me with shining breast.

When light in the realms of space lay hidden,
When life was yet in the womb of time,
Ere flesh was fettered to fruits forbidden,
And souls were wedded to care and crime,
Was the course foreshaped for the future spirit—
A burden of folly, a void of merit—
That would fain the wisdom of stars inherit,
And cannot fathom the seas sublime?

Under the sea or the soil (what matter?
The sea and the soil are under the sun),
As in the former days in the latter,
The sleeping or waking is known of none.
Surely the sleeper shall not awaken
To griefs forgotten or joys forsaken,
For the price of all things given and taken,
The sum of all things done and undone.

Shall we count offences or coin excuses,
Or weigh with scales the soul of a man,
Whom a strong hand binds and a sure hand looses,
Whose light is a spark and his life a span?
The seed he sow'd or the soil he cumber'd,
The time he served or the space he slumber'd,
Will it profit a man when his days are number'd,
Or his deeds since the days of his life began?

One, glad because of the light, saith, "Shall not
The righteous Judge of all the earth do right,
For behold the sparrows on the house-tops fall not
Save as seemeth to Him good in His sight?"
And this man's joy shall have no abiding,
Through lights departing and lives dividing,
He is soon as one in the darkness hiding,
One loving darkness rather than light.

A little season of love and laughter,
Of light and life, and pleasure and pain,
And a horror of outer darkness after,
And dust returneth to dust again.
Then the lesser life shall be as the greater,
And the lover of life shall join the hater,
And the one thing cometh sooner or later,
And no one knoweth the loss or gain.

Love of my life! we had lights in season—
Hard to part from, harder to keep—
We had strength to labour and souls to reason,
And seed to scatter and fruits to reap.
Though time estranges and fate disperses,

We have HAD our loves and our loving mercies;
Though the gifts of the light in the end are curses,
Yet bides the gift of the darkness—sleep!

See! girt with tempest and wing'd with thunder,
And clad with lightning and shod with sleet,
The strong winds treading the swift waves sunder
The flying rollers with frothy feet.
One gleam like a bloodshot sword-blade swims on
The sky-line, staining the green gulf crimson,
A death stroke fiercely dealt by a dim sun,
That strikes through his stormy winding-sheet.

Oh! brave white horses! you gather and gallop,
The storm sprite loosens the gusty reins;
Now the stoutest ship were the frailest shallop
In your hollow backs, or your high arch'd manes.
I would ride as never a man has ridden
In your sleepy, swirling surges hidden,
To gulfs foreshadow'd through straits forbidden,
Where no light wearies and no love wanes.

WOLF AND HOUND

You'll take my tale with a little salt,
But it needs none, nevertheless,
I was foil'd completely, fairly at fault,
Dishearten'd, too, I confess.

At the splitters' tent I had seen the track
Of horse-hoofs fresh on the sward,
And though Darby Lynch and Donovan Jack
(Who could swear through a ten-inch board)
Solemnly swore he had not been there,
I was just as sure that they lied,
For to Darby all that is foul was fair,
And Jack for his life was tried.

We had run him for seven miles and more
As hard as our nags could split;
At the start they were all too weary and sore,
And his was quite fresh and fit.
Young Marsden's pony had had enough
On the plain, where the chase was hot;
We breasted the swell of the Bittern's Bluff,
And Mark couldn't raise a trot;
When the sea, like a splendid silver shield,
To the south-west suddenly lay;
On the brow of the Beetle the chestnut reel'd,
And I bid good-bye to M'Crea --
And I was alone when the mare fell lame,
With a pointed flint in her shoe,
On the Stony Flats: I had lost the game,
And what was a man to do?

I turned away with no fixed intent
And headed for Hawthorndell;
I could neither eat in the splitters' tent,
Nor drink at the splitters' well;
I knew that they gloried in my mishap,
And I cursed them between my teeth --
A blood-red sunset through Brayton's Gap
Flung a lurid fire on the heath.
Could I reach the Dell? I had little reck,
And with scarce a choice of my own
I threw the reins on Miladi's neck --
I had freed her foot from the stone.
That season most of the swamps were dry,
And after so hard a burst
In the sultry noon of so hot a sky,
She was keen to appease her thirst --
Or by instinct urged or impelled by fate --
I care not to solve these things --
Certain it is that she took me straight
To the Warrigal water springs.

I can shut my eyes and recall the ground
As though it were yesterday --
With a shelf of the low, grey rocks girt round,
The springs in their basin lay;
Woods to the east and wolds to the north
In the sundown sullenly bloom'd;
Dead black on a curtain of crimson cloth
Large peaks to the westward loomed.
I led Miladi through weed and sedge,
She leisurely drank her fill;
There was something close to the water's edge,

And my heart with one leap stood still,
For a horse's shoe and a rider's boot
Had left clean prints on the clay;
Someone had watered his beast on foot.
'Twas he -- he had gone. Which way?
Then the mouth of the cavern faced me fair,
As I turned and fronted the rocks;
So, at last, I had pressed the wolf to his lair,
I had run to his earth the fox.

I thought so. Perhaps he was resting. Perhaps
He was waiting, watching for me.
I examined all my revolver caps,
I hitched my mare to a tree --
I had sworn to have him, alive or dead,
And to give him a chance was loth.
He knew his life had been forfeited --
He had even heard of my oath.
In my stocking'd soles to the shelf I crept,
I crawl'd safe into the cave --
All silent -- if he was there he slept
Not there. All dark as the grave.

Through the crack I could hear the leaden hiss!
See the livid face through the flame!
How strange it seems that a man should miss
When his life depends on his aim!
There couldn't have been a better light
For him, nor a worse for me.
We were coop'd up, caged like beasts for a fight,
And dumb as dumb beasts were we.

Flash! flash! bang! bang! and we blazed away,
And the grey roof reddened and rang;
Flash! flash! and I felt his bullet flay
The tip of my ear. Flash! bang!
Bang! flash! and my pistol arm fell broke;
I struck with my left hand then --
Struck at a corpse through a cloud of smoke --
I had shot him dead in his den!

TO MY SISTER

Across the trackless seas I go,
No matter when or where,
And few my future lot will know,
And fewer still will care.
My hopes are gone, my time is spent,
I little heed their loss,
And if I cannot feel content,
I cannot feel remorse.

My parents bid me cross the flood,
My kindred frowned at me;
They say I have belied my blood,
And stained my pedigree.
But I must turn from those who chide,
And laugh at those who frown;
I cannot quench my stubborn pride,
Nor keep my spirits down.

I once had talents fit to win
Success in life's career,
And if I chose a part of sin,
My choice has cost me dear.
But those who brand me with disgrace
Will scarcely dare to say
They spoke the taunt before my face,
And went unscathed away.

My friends will miss a comrade's face,
And pledge me on the seas,
Who shared the wine-cup or the chase,
Or follies worse than these.

A careless smile, a parting glass,
A hand that waves adieu,
And from my sight they soon will pass,
And from my memory too.

I loved a girl not long ago,
And, till my suit was told,
I thought her breast as fair as snow,
'Twas very near as cold;
And yet I spoke, with feelings more
Of recklessness than pain,
Those words I never spoke before,
Nor never shall again.

Her cheek grew pale, in her dark eye
I saw the tear-drop shine;
Her red lips faltered in reply,
And then were pressed to mine.
A quick pulsation of the heart!
A flutter of the breath!
A smothered sob — and thus we part,
To meet no more till death.

And yet I may at times recall
Her memory with a sigh;
At times for me the tears may fall
And dim her sparkling eye.
But absent friends are soon forgot,
And in a year or less
'Twill doubtless be another's lot
Those very lips to press!

With adverse fate we best can cope
When all we prize has fled;
And where there's little left to hope,
There's little left to dread!
Oh, time glides ever quickly by!
Destroying all that's dear;
On earth there's little worth a sigh,
And nothing worth a tear!

What fears have I? What hopes in life?
What joys can I command?
A few short years of toil and strife
In a strange and distant land!
When green grass sprouts above this clay
(And that might be ere long),
Some friends may read these lines and say,
The world has judged him wrong.

There is a spot not far away
Where my young sister sleeps,
Who seems alive but yesterday,
So fresh her memory keeps;
For we have played in childhood there
Beneath the hawthorn's bough,
And bent our knee in childish prayer
I cannot utter now!

Of late so reckless and so wild,
That spot recalls to me
That I was once a laughing child,
As innocent as she;
And there, while August's wild flow'rs wave,

I wandered all alone,
Strewed blossoms on her little grave,
And knelt beside the stone.

I seem to have a load to bear,
A heavy, choking grief;
Could I have forced a single tear
I might have felt relief.
I think my hot and restless heart
Has scorched the channels dry,
From which those sighs of sorrow start
To moisten cheek and eye.

Sister, farewell! farewell once more
To every youthful tie!
Friends! parents! kinsmen! native shore!
To each and all good-bye!
And thoughts which for the moment seem
To bind me with a spell,
Ambitious hope! love's boyish dream!
To you a last farewell!

A HUNTING SONG

Here's a health to every sportsman, be he stableman or lord,
If his heart be true, I care not what his pocket may afford;
And may he ever pleasantly each gallant sport pursue,
If he takes his liquor fairly, and his fences fairly, too.

He cares not for the bubbles of Fortune's fickle tide,
Who like Bendigo can battle, and like Olliver can ride.
He laughs at those who caution, at those who chide he'll frown,
As he clears a five-foot paling, or he knocks a peeler down.

The dull, cold world may blame us, boys! but what care we the while,
If coral lips will cheer us, and bright eyes on us smile?
For beauty's fond caresses can most tenderly repay
The weariness and trouble of many an anxious day.

Then fill your glass, and drain it, too, with all your heart and soul,
To the best of sports — The Fox-hunt, The Fair Ones, and The Bowl,
To a stout heart in adversity through every ill to steer,
And when Fortune smiles a score of friends like those around us here.

AN EXILE'S FAREWELL

The ocean heaves around us still
With long and measured swell,
The autumn gales our canvas fill,
Our ship rides smooth and well.
The broad Atlantic's bed of foam
Still breaks against our prow;
I shed no tears at quitting home,
Nor will I shed them now!

Against the bulwarks on the poop
I lean, and watch the sun
Behind the red horizon stoop —
His race is nearly run.
Those waves will never quench his light,
O'er which they seem to close,
To-morrow he will rise as bright
As he this morning rose.

How brightly gleams the orb of day
Across the trackless sea!
How lightly dance the waves that play
Like dolphins in our lee!
The restless waters seem to say,
In smothered tones to me,
How many thousand miles away
My native land must be!

Speak, Ocean! is my Home the same
Now all is new to me? —
The tropic sky's resplendent flame,
The vast expanse of sea?

Does all around her, yet unchanged,
The well-known aspect wear?
Oh! can the leagues that I have ranged
Have made no difference there?

How vivid Recollection's hand
Recalls the scene once more!
I see the same tall poplars stand
Beside the garden door;
I see the bird-cage hanging still;
And where my sister set
The flowers in the window-sill —
Can they be living yet?

Let woman's nature cherish grief,
I rarely heave a sigh
Before emotion takes relief
In listless apathy;
While from my pipe the vapours curl
Towards the evening sky,
And 'neath my feet the billows whirl
In dull monotony!

The sky still wears the crimson streak
Of Sol's departing ray,
Some briny drops are on my cheek,
'Tis but the salt sea spray!
Then let our barque the ocean roam,
Our keel the billows plough;
I shed no tears at quitting home,
Nor will I shed them now!

A FRAGMENT

They say that poison-sprinkled flowers
Are sweeter in perfume
Than when, untouched by deadly dew,
They glowed in early bloom.

They say that men condemned to die
Have quaffed the sweetened wine
With higher relish than the juice
Of the untampered vine.

They say that in the witch's song,
Though rude and harsh it be,
There blends a wild, mysterious strain
Of weirdest melody.

And I believe the devil's voice
Sinks deeper in our ear
Than any whisper sent from Heaven,
However sweet and clear.

HENRY KENDALL

Thomas Henry Kendall was an Australian author and bush poet mainly known for his poems and tales set in a natural environment. He appears never to have used his first name — his three volumes of verse were all published under "Henry Kendall." His verse was a triumph over a life of adversity. He was one of the first Australian poets to draw inspiration from the country's life, scenery, and traditions. In the beginnings of Australian poetry, the names of two other men stand with his -- Adam Lindsay Gordon, of English parentage and education, and Charles Harpur, born in Australia a generation earlier than Kendall. Harpur's work shows fitful gleams of poetic fire suggestive of more extraordinary achievement had the circumstances of his life been more favorable. Kendall, whose lot was scarcely more fortunate, is a true singer; his songs remain and are likely long to remain attractive to poetry lovers.

THE LAST OF HIS TRIBE

He crouches, and buries his face on his knees,
And hides in the dark of his hair;
For he cannot look up to the storm-smitten trees,
Or think of the loneliness there -
Of the loss and the loneliness there.

The wallaroos grope through the tufts of the grass,
And turn to their coverts for fear;
But he sits in the ashes and lets them pass
Where the boomerangs sleep with the spear -
With the nullah, the sling and the spear.

Uloola, behold him! The thunder that breaks
On the tops of the rocks with the rain,
And the wind which drives up with the salt of the lakes,
Have made him a hunter again -
A hunter and fisher again.

For his eyes have been full with a smouldering thought;
But he dreams of the hunts of yore,
And of foes that he sought, and of fights that he fought
With those who will battle no more -
Who will go to the battle no more.

It is well that the water which tumbles and fills
Goes moaning and moaning along;
For an echo rolls out from the sides of the hills,
And he starts at a wonderful song -
At the sound of a wonderful song.

And he sees through the rents of the scattering fogs

The corroboree warlike and grim,
And the lubra who sat by the fire on the logs,
To watch, like a mourner, for him -
Like a mother and mourner for him.

Will he go in his sleep from these desolate lands,
Like a chief, to the rest of his race,
With the honey-voiced woman who beckons and stands,
And gleams like a dream in his face -
Like a marvellous dream in his face?

BELL BIRDS

By channels of coolness the echoes are calling,
And down the dim gorges I hear the creek falling;
It lives in the mountain, where moss and the sedges
Touch with their beauty the banks and the ledges;
Through brakes of the cedar and sycamore bowers
Struggles the light that is love to the flowers.
And, softer than slumber, and sweeter than singing,
The notes of the bell-birds are running and ringing.

The silver-voiced bell-birds, the darlings of day-time,
They sing in September their songs of the May-time.
When shadows wax strong and the thunder-bolts hurtle,
They hide with their fear in the leaves of the myrtle;
When rain and the sunbeams shine mingled together
They start up like fairies that follow fair weather,
And straightway the hues of their feathers unfolden
Are the green and the purple, the blue and the golden.

October, the maiden of bright yellow tresses,
Loiters for love in these cool wildernesses;
Loiters knee-deep in the grasses to listen,
Where dripping rocks gleam and the leafy pools glisten.
Then is the time when the water-moons splendid
Break with their gold, and are scattered or blended
Over the creeks, till the woodlands have warning
Of songs of the bell-bird and wings of the morning.

Welcome as waters unkissed by the summers
Are the voices of bell-birds to thirsty far-comers.
When fiery December sets foot in the forest,
And the need of the wayfarer presses the sorest,

Pent in the ridges for ever and ever.
The bell-birds direct him to spring and to river,
With ring and with ripple, like runnels whose torrents
Are toned by the pebbles and leaves in the currents.

Often I sit, looking back to a childhood
Mixt with the sights and the sounds of the wildwood,
Longing for power and the sweetness to fashion
Lyrics with beats like the heart-beats of passion --
Songs interwoven of lights and of laughters
Borrowed from bell-birds in far forest rafters;
So I might keep in the city and alleys
The beauty and strength of the deep mountain valleys,
Charming to slumber the pain of my losses
With glimpses of creeks and a vision of mosses.

SILENT TEARS

What bitter sorrow courses down
Yon mourner's faded cheek?
Those scalding drops betray a grief
Within, too full to speak.
Outspoken words cannot express
The pangs, the pains of years;
They're ne'er so deep or eloquent
As are those silent tears.
Here is a wound that in the breast
Must canker, hid'n from sight;
Though all without seems sunny day,
Within 'Tis ever night.
Yet sometimes from this secret source
The gloomy truth appears;
The wind's dark dungeon must have vent
If but in silent tears.

The world may deem from outward looks
That heart is hard and cold;
But oh! could they the mantle lift
What sorrows would be told!
Then, only then, the truth would show
Which most the bosom sears:
The pain portrayed by burning words
Or that by—silent tears.

BILL THE BULLOCK-DRIVER

The Leaders of millions, the lords of the lands,
Who sway the wide world with their will
And shake the great globe with the strength of their hands,
Flash past us—unnoticed by Bill.
The elders of science who measure the spheres
And weigh the vast bulk of the sun—
Who see the grand lights beyond aeons of years,
Are less than a bullock to one.

The singers that sweeten all time with their song—
Pure voices that make us forget
Humanity's drama of marvellous wrong—
To Bill are as mysteries yet.

By thunders of battle and nations uphurled,
Bill's sympathies never were stirred:
The helmsmen who stand at the wheel of the world
By him are unknown and unheard.

What trouble has Bill for the ruin of lands,
Or the quarrels of temple and throne,
So long as the whip that he holds in his hands
And the team that he drives are his own?

As straight and as sound as a slab without crack,
Our Bill is a king in his way;
Though he camps by the side of a shingle track,
And sleeps on the bed of his dray.

A whip-lash to him is as dear as a rose
Would be to a delicate maid;

He carries his darlings wherever he goes,
In a pocket-book tattered and frayed.

The joy of a bard when he happens to write
A song like the song of his dream
Is nothing at all to our hero's delight
In the pluck and the strength of his team.

For the kings of the earth, for the faces august
Of princes, the millions may shout;
To Bill, as he lumbers along in the dust,
A bullock's the grandest thing out.

His four-footed friends are the friends of his choice—
No lover is Bill of your dames;
But the cattle that turn at the sound of his voice
Have the sweetest of features and names.

A father's chief joy is a favourite son,
When he reaches some eminent goal,
But the pride of Bill's heart is the hairy-legged one
That pulls with a will at the pole.

His dray is no living, responsible thing,
But he gives it the gender of life;
And, seeing his fancy is free in the wing,
It suits him as well as a wife.

He thrives like an Arab. Between the two wheels
Is his bedroom, where, lying up-curled,
He thinks for himself, like a sultan, and feels
That his home is the best in the world.

For, even though cattle, like subjects, will break
At times from the yoke and the band,
Bill knows how to act when his rule is at stake,
And is therefore a lord of the land.

Of course he must dream; but be sure that his dreams,
If happy, must compass, alas!
Fat bullocks at feed by improbable streams,
Knee-deep in improbable grass.

No poet is Bill, for the visions of night
To him are as visions of day;
And the pipe that in sleep he endeavours to light
Is the pipe that he smokes on the dray.

To the mighty, magnificent temples of God,
In the hearts of the dominant hills,
Bill's eyes are as blind as the fire-blackened clod
That burns far away from the rills.

Through beautiful, bountiful forests that screen
A marvel of blossoms from heat—
Whose lights are the mellow and golden and green—
Bill walks with irreverent feet.

The manifold splendours of mountain and wood
By Bill like nonentities slip;
He loves the black myrtle because it is good
As a handle to lash to his whip.

And thus through the world, with a swing in his tread,
Our hero self-satisfied goes;

With his cabbage-tree hat on the back of his head,
And the string of it under his nose.

Poor bullocky Bill! In the circles select
Of the scholars he hasn't a place;
But he walks like a man, with his forehead erect,
And he looks at God's day in the face.

For, rough as he seems, he would shudder to wrong
A dog with the loss of a hair;
And the angels of shine and superlative song
See his heart and the deity there.

Few know him, indeed; but the beauty that glows
In the forest is loveliness still;
And Providence helping the life of the rose
Is a Friend and a Father to Bill.

THE MUSE OF AUSTRALIA

Where the pines with the eagles are nestled in rifts,
And the torrent leaps down to the surges,
I have followed her, clambering over the cliffs,
By the chasms and moon-haunted verges.
I know she is fair as the angels are fair,
For have I not caught a faint glimpse of her there;
A glimpse of her face and her glittering hair,
And a hand with the Harp of Australia?

I never can reach you, to hear the sweet voice
So full with the music of fountains!
Oh! when will you meet with that soul of your choice,
Who will lead you down here from the mountains?
A lyre-bird lit on a shimmering space;
It dazzled mine eyes and I turned from the place,
And wept in the dark for a glorious face,
And a hand with the Harp of Australia!

SONG OF THE CATTLE HUNTERS

While the morning light beams on the fern-matted streams,
And the water-pools flash in its glow,
Down the ridges we fly, with a loud ringing cry —
Down the ridges and gullies we go!
And the cattle we hunt — they are racing in front,
With a roar like the thunder of waves,
As the beat and the beat of our swift horses' feet
Start the echoes away from their caves!
As the beat and the beat
Of our swift horses' feet
Start the echoes away from their caves!

Like a wintry shore that the waters ride o'er,
All the lowlands are filling with sound;
For swiftly we gain where the herds on the plain,
Like a tempest, are tearing the ground!
And we'll follow them hard to the rails of the yard,
O'er the gulches and mountain-tops grey,
Where the beat and the beat of our swift horses' feet
Will die with the echoes away!
Where the beat and the beat
Of our swift horses' feet
Will die with the echoes away!

SEPTEMBER IN AUSTRALIA

Grey Winter hath gone, like a wearisome guest,
And, behold, for repayment,
September comes in with the wind of the West
And the Spring in her raiment!
The ways of the frost have been filled of the flowers,
While the forest discovers
Wild wings, with the halo of hyaline hours,
And the music of lovers.

September, the maid with the swift, silver feet!
She glides, and she graces
The valleys of coolness, the slopes of the heat,
With her blossomy traces;
Sweet month, with a mouth that is made of a rose,
She lightens and lingers
In spots where the harp of the evening glows,
Attuned by her fingers.

The stream from its home in the hollow hill slips
In a darling old fashion;
And the day goeth down with a song on its lips
Whose key-note is passion;
Far out in the fierce, bitter front of the sea
I stand, and remember
Dead things that were brothers and sisters of thee,
Resplendent September.

The West, when it blows at the fall of the noon
And beats on the beaches,
Is filled with a tender and tremulous tune
That touches and teaches;

The stories of Youth, of the burden of Time,
And the death of Devotion,
Come back with the wind, and are themes of the rhyme
In the waves of the ocean.

We, having a secret to others unknown,
In the cool mountain-mosses,
May whisper together, September, alone
Of our loves and our losses.
One word for her beauty, and one for the grace
She gave to the hours;
And then we may kiss her, and suffer her face
To sleep with the flowers.

~~~~~~

Oh, season of changes — of shadow and shine —
September the splendid!
My song hath no music to mingle with thine,
And its burden is ended;
But thou, being born of the winds and the sun,
By mountain, by river,
Mayst lighten and listen, and loiter and run,
With thy voices for ever.

A MOUNTAIN SPRING

Peace hath an altar there. The sounding feet
Of thunder and the wildering wings of rain
Against fire-rifted summits flash and beat,
And through grey upper gorges swoop and strain;
But round that hallowed mountain-spring remain,
Year after year, the days of tender heat,
And gracious nights whose lips with flowers are sweet,
And filtered lights, and lutes of soft refrain.
A still, bright pool. To men I may not tell
The secrets that its heart of water knows,
The story of a loved and lost repose;
Yet this I say to cliff and close-leaved dell:
A fitful spirit haunts yon limpid well,
Whose likeness is the faithless face of Rose.

MARY GILMORE

Dame Mary Jean Gilmore DBE was an Australian writer and journalist known for prolific contributions to Australian literature and the broader national discourse. She wrote both prose and poetry. Her first collection of poetry was published in 1910. Marri'd and other Verses had been written partly during her time at the Cosme colony in Paraguay and when she had returned to Australia. It began her career as one the county's most influential and widely read poets as she appealed to everyday people with her verses about the vagaries of ordinary life. Gilmore was a highly vocal and much-loved voice in Australia, and her birthdays were often celebrated by the literary community and regular, everyday folk who liked what she said. She died in 1962 at the grand old age of 97 and was given one of the first state funerals for a writer since 1922.

MARRI'D

IT'S singin' in an' out,
An' feelin' full of grace;
Here 'n' there, up an' down,
An' round about th' place.

It's rollin' up your sleeves,
An' whit'nin' up the hearth,
An' scrubbin' out th' floors,
An' sweepin' down th' path;

It's bakin' tarts an' pies,
An' shinin' up th' knives;
An' feelin' 's if some days
Was worth a thousand lives.

It's watchin' out th' door,
An' watchin' by th' gate;
An' watchin' down th' road,
An' wonderin' why he's late;

An' feelin' anxious-like,
For fear there's something wrong;
An' wonderin' why he's kep',
An' why he takes so long.

It's comin' back inside
An' sittin' down a spell,
To sort of make believe
You're thinkin' things is well.

It's gettin' up again

An' wand'rin' in an' out;
An' feelin' wistful-like,
Not knowin' what about;

An' flushin' all at once,
An' smilin' just so sweet,
An' feelin' real proud
The place is fresh an' neat.

An' feelin' awful glad
Like them that watch'd Silo'm;
An' everything because
A man is comin' Home!

MARY HANNAY FOOTT

Mary Hannay Foott was a Scottish-born Australian poet and editor. She is well remembered for a bush-ballad poem, "Where the Pelican Builds." Mary Hannay Foott was born in Glasgow to a merchant, James Black, and his wife, née Grant. The family moved to Australia in 1853 and lived for some years at Mordialloc, near Melbourne, where Mary attended Miss Harper's school. She became one of the first students at Melbourne's National Gallery of Victoria Art School. Foott's published verse was small in quantity but usually of good quality—her Poem "Where the Pelican Builds" appears in most Australian anthologies.

WHERE THE PELICAN BUILDS

The horses were ready,
The rails were down,
But the riders lingered still
One had a parting word to say
And one had his pipe to fill

They had told us of pastures
Wide and green,
To be sought past the sunsets' glow,
Of rifts in the ranges by opals lit
And gold 'neath the rivers flow

The creek at the ford
Was but fetlock deep,
When we watched them crossing there,
The rains have replenished it thrice since then
And thrice has the rocks lain bare.

But the waters of hope
Have flower and fled,
And never from blue hills breast,
Came back, by the sun and sand devoured
Where the Pelican builds its nest.

IN THE LAND OF DREAMS

A Bridle-path in the tangled mallee,
With blossoms unnamed and unknown bespread,—
And two who ride through its leafy alley,—
But never the sound of a horse's tread.
And one by one whilst the foremost rider
Puts back the boughs which have grown apace,—
And side by side where the track is wider,—
Together they come to the olden place.

To the leaf-dyed pool whence the mallards flattered,
Or ever the horses had paused to drink;
Where the word was said and the vow was uttered
That brighten for ever its weedy brink.

And Memory closes her sad recital,—
In Fate's cold eyes there are kindly gleams,—
While for one brief moment of blest requital,—
The parted have met,—in the Land of Dreams.

NO MESSAGE

She heard the story of the end,
Each message, too, she heard;
And there was one for every friend;
For her alone — no word.

And shall she bear a heavier heart,
And deem his love was fled;
Because his soul from earth could part
Leaving her name unsaid?

No — No! — Though neither sign nor sound
A parting thought expressed —
Not heedless passed the Homeward-Bound
Of her he loved the best.

Of voyage-perils, bravely borne,
He would not tell the tale;
Of shattered planks and canvas torn,
And war with wind and gale.

He waited till the light-house star
Should rise against the sky;
And from the mainland, looming far,
The forest scents blow by.

He hoped to tell — assurance sweet! —
That pain and grief were o'er —
What blessings haste the soul to meet,
Ere yet within the door.

Then one farewell he thought to speak

When all the rest were past —
As in the parting-hour we seek
The dearest hand the last.

And while for this delaying but
To see Heaven's opening Gate —
Lo, it received him — and was shut —
Ere he could say "I wait."

THE FUTURE OF AUSTRALIA

Sing us the Land of the Southern Sea,—
The land we have called our own;
Tell us what harvest there shall be
From the seed that we have sown.
We love the legends of olden days,
The songs of the wind and wave;
And border ballads and minstrel lays,
And the poems Shakespeare gave,—

The fireside carols and battle rhymes,
And romaunt of the knightly ring;
And the chant with hint of cathedral chimes,—
Of him "made blind to sing."

The tears they tell of our brethren wept,—
Their praise is our fathers' fame;
They sing of the seas our navies swept,—
Of the shrines that lent us flame.

But the Past is past,—with all its pride,—
And its ways are not our ways.
We watch the flow of a fresher tide
And the dawn of newer days.

Sing us the Isle of the Southern Sea,—
The land we have called our own;
Tell us what harvest there shall be
From the seed that we have sown.

I see the Child we are tending now
To a queenly stature grown;

The jewels of empire on her brow,
And the purple round her thrown.

She feeds her household plenteously
From the granaries we have filled;
Her vintage is gathered in with glee
From the fields our toil has tilled.

The Old World's outcast starvelings feast,—
Ungrudged,—on her corn and wine;
The gleaners are welcome, from west and east,
Where her autumn sickles shine.

She clothes her people in silk and wool,—
Whose warp and whose woof we spun;
And sons and daughters are hers to rule;
And of slaves,—she has not one!

There are herds of hers on a thousand hills!
There are fleecy flocks untold?
No foreign conquest her coffer fills,—
She has streams whose sands are gold!

She shall not scramble for falling crowns,—
No theft her soul shall soil,—
So rich in rivers, so dowered with downs,—
She shall have no need of spoil!

But if,—wronged or menaced,—she shall stand
Where the battle-surges swell,—
Be a sword from Heaven in her swarthy hand
Like the sword of La Pucelle!

If there be ever so base a foe
As to speak of a time-cleansed stain,—
To say, "She was cradled long ago,
'Mid clank of the convict's chain."

Ask,—as the taunt in his teeth is hurled,—
"What lineage sprang SHE from
Who was Empress, once, of the Pagan World
And the Queen of Christendom?"

When the toilsome years of her youth are o'er,
And her children round her throng;
They shall learn from her of the sage's lore,
And her lips shall teach them song.

Then of those in the dust who dwell,
May there kindly mention be,
When the birds that build in the branches tell
Of the planting of the tree.

THE MASSACRE OF THE BARDS

The sunlight from the sky is swept,

But, over Snowdon's summit kept,

One brand of cloud yet burns,—

By ghostly hands far out of sight,

Held, glowing, in the even-light,—

As Fate still keeps the weapon bright

That lingers and returns.

.....

O day of slaughter! Day of woe!—

But once,—a thousand years ago,—

Such day has Britain seen;

When blushed her hoary hills with shame

At Mona's sacrifice of flame;

While shrieks from out the burning came

Across the strait between.

Death-helping day!—That couldst not find

One weeping cloud to hide behind!—

Cursed day whose light was given

For search-mate to the Saxon sword

Through coverts that our rocks afford,—

While Edward's godless minions poured

The blood of the unshriven!

.....

Ill fare we when the trees are rent,

Whose friendly shelter erst was lent

In sun, and wind, and rain.

Ill fare we when the thunder-shocks

Let loose the torrents from their rocks,

To sweep away the mountain-flocks,

And flood the standing grain.

But where the forest-giants groan,—

By winds that waste the woods o'erthrown,—
New saplings blithely spring!—
Sank herd and harvest 'neath the tide?—
There's bleating on the mountain-side;
O'er cornfields, ere the dew has dried
To-morrow's lark shall sing!

Sore sighs the land when she has need
The dragon-jaws of war to feed
With those who love her best;
And long shall Cambria's tears be shed
For him who late her armies led,—
Llewellyn,—whose dissevered head
The Saxon crowned in jest!

Yet, in their stead whose blood is spilt,
Newcomers seize the sword's warm hilt,—
Or o'er it reach the ground!—
Llewellyn!—every night-watch drear
With grief for thee,—brings morning near;
That morn when Arthur shall appear,—
Once more our leader crowned!

But when the blood of bards is poured,
Who gathers their forgotten hoard
From memories sealed by fate?—
What daring songster e'er shall soar
For us to Heaven's death-guarded door,—
And tell thereafter of the store
That glimmers through the grate?

When Famine's empty hand is filled,—

When years the shattered oaks rebuild,—
Shall heroes spring again,
Brave spirits of the past to greet
Who rise at minstrel-summons sweet,—
When bards the olden tales repeat
Of Britain's mighty slain?—

Nay,—by the harps our fathers heard
No more shall Britain's heart be stirred,—
Lost is the ancient lore!—
Spent is the breath of song, that fanned
Freedom's low fires!—The bard's light hand,—
Whose beckoning brought the martial band,—
Shall seek the strings no more!

HAPPY DAYS

A fringe of rushes — one green line
Upon a faded plain;
A silver streak of water-shine —
Above, tree-watchers twain.
It was our resting-place awhile,
And still, with backward gaze,
We say: "'Tis many a weary mile —
But there were happy days."

And shall no ripple break the sand
Upon our farther way?
Or reedy ranks all knee-deep stand?
Or leafy tree-tops sway?
The gold of dawn is surely met
In sunset's lavish blaze;
And — in horizons hidden yet —
There shall be happy days.

UP NORTH

Into Thy hands let me fall, 0 Lord,—
Not into the hands of men,—
And she thinned the ranks of the savage horde
Till they shrank to the mangrove fen.
In a rudderless boat, with a scanty store
Of food for the fated three,—
With her babe and her stricken servitor
She fled to the open sea.

Oh, days of dolor and nights of drouth,
While she watched for a sail in vain,
Or the tawny tinge of a river mouth,
Or the rush of the tropic rain.

The valiant woman! Her feeble oar
Sufficed, and her fervent prayer
Was heard, though she reached but a barren shore,
And died with her darling there.

For the demons of murder and foul disgrace
On her hearthstone dared not light;
But the Angel of Womanhood held the place,
And its site is a holy site.

TO HENRY THE FIFTH

My youth was passing, Sire, whilst you among
The cradle-wrappings slept; my morning-song
Sung o'er your pillow. Winds of heaven have thrown
Us both, since then, on heights apart and lone.
Heights! For misfortune drear, our destined land,
So thunder-scarred, a-nigh to heaven must stand!
The north and south are nearer than our ways
Are near to one another; and Fate lays
The purple round you, and has not withheld
Our France's sceptre-dazzlements of eld.
I, crowned with silver hairs, say—praising you—
"Well done!" That man is to his manhood true
Who bravely, at his own behest, will do
High deeds of self -undoing; will forego
All—all—save immemorial Honour;—though
She seem to earthlier eyes a phantom, more
Will follow her (as erst in Elsinore
One faithful heart obeyed the beckoning ghost),
Nor stoop to buy a kingdom at her cost.
That you are aught save honest, none may say;
The Lily must be white—all white—for aye.
A Bourbon can but reign as Capet's heir,
Or waive his kingship. History is aware
Of wrecks enough—of changing battles' din—
Of those who grandly lose, or basely win!
Better with honour, Prince, the throne to quit.
Than, where St. Louis sat, dishonoured sit!

IN THE SOUTH PACIFIC

A vision of a savage land,
A glimpse of cloud-ringed seas;
A moonlit deck, a murderous hand;—
No more, no more of these!

No more! how heals the tender flesh,
Once torn by savage beast?
The wound, re-opening, bleeds afresh,
Each season at the least!

O day, for dawn of thee how prayed
The spirit, sore distressed;
Thy latest beams, upslanting, made
A pathway for the blest.

And robes, new-donned, of the redeemed,
Gleamed white past grief's dark pall:
So this, a day of death which seemed,
A birthday let us call.

Remembering, such day as this,
A soul from flesh was shriven,
By death, God's messenger of bliss;
A spirit entered Heaven.

Thy dying head no loving breast
Upheld, O early slain;
But soon, mid welcoming saints, 'twas prest
Where God's own Child has lain!

Though none at death broke Bread for thee,
Or poured the Sacred Wine;

Thou, nourished at His Board, dost see
The Substance of the Sign.

We mourned thee! Heaven's new born, and rich
Past all our prayers could claim,
Secure in blessedness, of which
We have not learnt the name.

JOHN FARRELL

John Farrell was an Argentinean-born Australian poet and journalist. He had a strong interest in literature, and in 1878, he produced a small collection of poems under the title Ephemera: An Iliad of Albury. This was described as a "satirical epic" and perhaps Farrell's attempt to produce something on ancient classical lines. His work frequently appeared in the Sydney Bulletin and, in 1882, was published. While never ascending to the heights of greatness, he was a competent writer and popular with readers and literary critics. Like many immigrants at the time, he wrote about both the old world left behind and the new one recently discovered.

AUSTRALIA

O Radiant Land! o'er whom the Sun's first dawning
Fell brightest when God said " Let there be Light;"'
O'er whom the day hung out its bluest awning
Whitening to wondrous deeps of stars by night—
O Land exultant! on whose brow reposes
A queenlier coronal than has been wrought
From light of pearls and bloom of Eastern roses
In all the workshops of high Poet-thought!—

O thou who hast, thy splendid hair entwining,
A toil-won wreath where are no blood-splashed bays,
Who standest in a stainless vestment shining
Before the eyes and lips of love and praise—
O wrought of old in Orient clime and sunny,
With all His richest bounties graced and decked;
Thy heart all virgin gold, thy breath all honey,
Supremest work of greatest Architect!—

O Land of widest hope, of promise boundless,
Why wert thou hidden in a dark, strange sea
To wait through ages, fruitless, scentless, soundless,
Till from thy slumber men should waken thee?—
Why did'st thou lie, with ear that never hearkened
The sounds without, the cries of strife and play,
Like some sweet child within a chamber darkened
Left sleeping far into a troubled day?—

What opiate sealed thine eyes while all the others
Grew tired and faint in East and West and North ;
Why did'st thou dream until thy joyful brothers
Found where thou wast, and led thee smiling forth?—

Why did'st thou mask the happy face thou wearest?
Why wert thou veiled from all the eager eyes?
Why left so long, O first of lands and fairest,
Beneath the tent of unconjectured skies?

We know thy secret. In the awful ages
When there was silence and the world was white,
Ere yet on the recording volume's pages
The stern-browed Angel had begun to write;
Ere yet from Eden the sad feet had wandered
Or yet was sin or any spilth of blood,
August in judgment, God the Father pondered
Upon His work, and saw that it was good—

The Sovereign of suns and stars, the thunder
Of whose dread Power we cannot understand,
Sate throned and musing on the shining wonder
Of this new world within His hollowed hand,
With high sad eyes, like one that saw a vision—
And spake "Lo! this My gift is fair to see,
But Pride will mar the glory, and derision
Of many feet that will not follow Me.

"I give my creatures shields of hope and warning;
I set in fruitful ways of peace their first;
But even these will turn from Me, and scorning
My council, hearken to the Voice Accurst;
And sin, and pain, and death will make invasion
Of this abode, and from a world undone
To Heaven will sound the moans of expiation
They wring from Him, My well-beloved Son.

"And yet again will they, with eyes unheeding
His sacrifice, uplift their guilty hands
Against their brethren, and with rage exceeding
And lust, and vengeance, desolate the lands.
But this one land," so mused He, the Creator,
"This will I bless and hide from all the woe,
That worthier among men, in ages later
May find it pure, and, haply, hold it so."

Then, sweet Australia, fell a benediction
Of sleep upon thee, where no wandering breath
Might come to tell thee of the loud affliction
Of cursing tongues and clamouring hosts of death;
And with the peace of His great lore around thee,
And rest that clashing ages could not break,
Strong-sighted eyes of English seekers found thee,
Strong English voices cried to thee "Awake!"

For them a continent undreamed of, peerless,
A realm for happier sons of theirs to be,
One land preserved unspotted, bloodless, tearless,
Beyond the rim of an enchanted sea
Lay folded in the soft compelling languor
Of warm south airs, like an awaiting bride,
While strife, and hate, and culminating anger
Raged through the far-off nations battle-dyed.

Here were no dreadful vestiges imprinted
With evil messages and brands of Cain,
No mounds of death or walls of refuge dinted
With signs that Christ had lived and died in rain;
No chill memorials here proclaimed the story

Of kingships stricken for and murders done;
Here was a marvel and a separate glory,
One land whose history had not begun!

One unsown garden, fenced by sea-crags sterile,
Whose iron breasts flung back the thundering waves,
From all the years of fierce unrest and peril,
And slaves, and lords, and broken blades, and graves;
One gracious freehold for the free, where only
Soft dusky feet fell, reaching not thy sleep;
One field inviolate, untroubled, lonely,
Across the dread of the uncharted deep!

O dear and fair! awakened from thy sleeping
So late! The world is breaking into noon;
The eyes that all the morn were dim with weeping
Smile through the tears that will cease dropping soon!
Thine have no tears in them for olden sorrow,
Thou hast no heartache for a ruined past;
From bright to-day to many a bright to-morrow
Shall be thy way, O first of lands and last!

THE LAST BULLET

Since the first human eyes saw the first timid
stars break through Heaven and shine,
Surely never a man was bowed down with
the cross of a curse such as mine;
They of all the dead millions of millions
whose dust whirls and flees in the wind,
Who were born helpless heirs of the hate
of a fate that is bitter and blind—

All whose lives pain has smitten with
fire since God first set the sun to its
course—
What have they known of woe like to mine?
What of grief? Of despair? Of remorse?
Oh! to cancel one hour of my past!
Oh! to shut out all thought, to forget,
Then go forth as a leper to die in hot wastes!
Listen! Over us yet,

Her and me, in the heart of the North,
hang the glamour of Love at its height,
Joy of things unperceived of the rest,
holy hours of unwaning delight;
Joy of selfless devotion to each in each heart;
joy of guiding the feet
Of our babe, our one daughter, our May,
by three summers of childhood made sweet!

I had dared overmuch in the battle for wealth,
I had ventured alone
Upon verdurous tracts that lay fronting

the edge of a desert unknown;
Fifty miles further out than the nearest
I chanced on a green width of plain,
In a time when the earth was made glad
by a grey year of bountiful rain;

Fifty miles from Maconochie's Gap.
They had warned me. Some three years gone by,
In a night when the flames of his home
reddened far up the heights of the sky,
With a hard ragged spear through his heart,
and a tomahawk blade in his head,
Lay the Master, in death, and his wife—
Ah! how better had she, too, lain dead !
Dark the tale is to tell, yet it was but a cruel resentment of wrong,
The fierce impulse of those who were weak,

for revenge upon those who were strong—
Cattle speared at the first, blacks shot down,
and the blood of their babes, even, shed;
Blood that stains the same hue as our own.
It is written, red blood will have red !

But an organised anger of whites swept the
bush with a fury unchained,
Till the dead seemed as thick as the trees,
and the black murdered corpses remained,
Till the black glutted crows scarce could
rise from their feast at the sound of a foot,
And the far-away camps through the nights
lay unlighted, and ghastly, and mute!

And a terror ran out through the tribes.
Since that devilish crime had been done;
Not a dusk stealthy savage had crossed
the wide bounds of Maconochie's run;
But the white sky in pitiless scorn
stared at waterless plains that implored
For the mercy of clouds that passed,
mocking them. "Vengeance is mine," said the Lord!

They had warned me. "Out yonder," they said,
"there's abundance of water and grass,
You've Brown's Ranges beside you, they
draw down and drain all the rain-clouds
that pass,
(We are outside the rainy belt here).
But remember the words we have said—
If you will go, prepare to have trouble;
take plenty of powder and lead!"

And I went, with my trustworthy helpers,
and lived through a desolate year
Of suspicions, and vigils, and hunger for
her of all dear ones most dear;
But a year crowned with utmost successes,
and crowned above all things in this,
That it brought her again to my side with
the gift of a new face to kiss!

And a blessedness came with her feet,
and our life was a prosperous peace,
And the years as they passed shed upon
us a fair meed of worldly increase;

But a thousand times better to me than
assurance of silver and gold
Was the measureless love of a wife,
mine for ever to have and to hold!

. Oh! the pang of remembering then!
Oh! could madness dishevel my mind,
Till I babbled of wry tangled things,
looking neither before nor behind!
But I shrink from the slumberless thought
of one deed, as the first of our race,
In the shame of his wrong-doing, crouched
from the light of God's terrible face!

We had hardly been vexed by the blacks
in our work, though all through the first year,
And the second, we stood upon guard with the disciplined earnest of fear,
But the summers and winters went by, and
the wild tribes gave never a proof
Of their hate, and our vigilance slept,
and security came to our roof.

So, unwarned, fell the night of my doom.
There was smoke in the west through the day,
And an hour after noon all the hands had
been mustered and sent out to stay
In its course the red wave that approached,
for the high grass was yellow and sere
With the withering breath of the dense
sullen heat of the last of the year.

They took rifles to shoot kangaroo, as it

chanced. My two darlings and I
Sat together at night by the door, with our
eyes on a fringe of the sky
Where the light of the late sunken sun was
replaced by a wide lurid glow,
Which pulsed high or grew pale as the fire
underneath it waxed fierce or waned low.

We had spoken glad-voiced of the time,
soon to come, when our exile would be
At an end, and our feet once again in the
quiet lands over the sea,
Till the large, lovely eyes of the child
felt their lids grow despotic. She drew
To her mother and slept in her arms, and
the new risen moon kissed the two.

I was looking beyond them to where the
broad columns of tree-shadows slept,
Stretching west twice the length of the
trees, when a horror of something that crept,
Something blacker than shade, through
the shade, struck my heart with a hammer
of ice,
And with eyeballs dilated and strained,
and hands clenched with the clench of a vice,

I leapt up; but a clear sudden whirr
cleaved the night, and with scarcely
a groan
From her lips, the white soul of our
child passed among the white souls at

the Throne!

"To the house!" with the dead and the

living, half dead, clasped before me,

I sprang

Through the strong door, and bolted

and barred it before, on the stillness,

out rang

A wild-volumed malignance of yells.

To have light might be death. In the dark,

On the floor, the poor mother groped

madly about the dead child for a spark

Of the hope of faint lingering life,

till the blood that was mine and her own

From the boomerang gash, warmed her

hands, and she knew that we two were alone!

Yell on yell of the monsters without!

crash of shutters behind!—but I knew

How the wall that divided was built;

that, at least, they could never get

through—

Crash of manifold blows on the door!

but, I knew too, how that had been made;

And I crawled to the corner and found

my revolvers, and hoarsely I said :

"Kiss me now, ere the worst comes to

pass, O most stricken and dearest of wives—

They will find out the window—I hold

in my hands but a dozen of lives.

In the storehouse the arms are,

God help us! Fold hands in the dark,

dear, and pray!"
But she sobbed from my feet,
"God forgets us, and I have forgotten
the way!"

Crash of spear through the window!
an answering flash with the message of lead
From my hand!—and dull answer to that
of a lean demon-form falling dead!
Crash on crash of a dozen of spears!
till they lay in a sheaf on the floor!—
Red rejoinder of fire, as the moonlight
revealed them— "But one bullet more!"

I had hissed to myself. But she heard me,
and seizing my arm, held it fast,
And a hard, altered voice that I knew
not at once, cried "Hold! I claim the last!
Dearest love, from your hand the divorce!
One last kiss till the Infinite Life—
Once again, on my lips! Hold it close,
and remember Maconochie's wife!"

By the white sickly light of a match,
she had bared that true bosom, all red
With the blood of her slain one.
I looked in her eyes. "God forgive me!"
I said ....
And the sound of the thing that I did
was repeated outside by a sound—
Not as awful to me the dread Trump,
when the time of my sentence comes round—

Rifle shots close at hand! devil-cries!

counter-cheers of the voices I knew!

They were back! I was saved! Lost! lost!

lost! Can the blood of the Saviour they slew

Upon Calvary's hill wash out her's

from my hands? For I trusted not God

To the full in the hour of my need,

and my lips will not cleave to the rod

Of his wrath, and I fall in the

sand with the weight of the cross that I bear—

Who has ever gone out with a burden of

pain, of remorse, of despair

Like to this? Let me stumble to death,

or through life—it is equally well;

Doubly damned, what can death bring

to me but translation from Hell unto Hell?

AUSTRALIA TO ENGLAND

What of the years of Englishmen?
What have they brought of growth and grace
Since mud-built London by its fen
Became the Briton's breeding-place?
What of the Village, where our blood
Was brewed by sires, half man, half brute,
In vessels of wild womanhood,
From blood of Saxon, Celt and Jute?

What are its gifts, this Harvest Home
Of English tilth and English cost,
Where fell the hamlet won by Rome
And rose the city that she lost?
O! terrible and grand and strange
Beyond all phantasy that gleams
When Hope, asleep, sees radiant Change
Come to her through the halls of dreams!

A heaving sea of life, that beats
Like England's heart of pride to-day,
And up from roaring miles of streets
Flings on the roofs its human spray;
And fluttering miles of flags aflow,
And cannon's voice, and boom of bell,
And seas of fire to-night, as though
A hundred cities flamed and fell;

While, under many a fair festoon
And flowering crescent, set ablaze
With all the dyes that English June
Can lend to deck a day of days,
And past where mart and palace rise,
And shrine and temple lift their spears,

Below five million misted eyes
Goes a grey Queen of Sixty Years --

Go lords, and servants of the lords
Of earth, with homage on their lips,
And kinsmen carrying English swords,
And offering England battle-ships;
And tribute-payers, on whose hands
Their English fetters scarce appear;
And gathered round from utmost lands
Ambassadors of Love and Fear!

Dim signs of greeting waved afar,
Far trumpets blown and flags unfurled,
And England's name an Avatar
Of light and sound throughout the world --
Hailed Empress among nations, Queen
Enthroned in solemn majesty,
On splendid proofs of what has been,
And presages of what will be!

For this your sons, foreseeing not
Or heeding not, the aftermath,
Because their strenuous hearts were hot
Went first on many a cruel path,
And, trusting first and last to blows,
Fed death with such as would gainsay
Their instant passing, or oppose
With talk of Right strength's right of way!

For this their names are on the stone
Of mountain spires, and carven trees
That stand in flickering wastes unknown
Wait with their dying messages;

When fire blasts dance with desert drifts
The English bones show white below,
And, not so white, when summer lifts
The counterpane of Yukon's snow.

Condemned by blood to reach for grapes
That hang in sight, however high,
Beyond the smoke of Asian capes,
The nameless, dauntless, dead ones lie;
And where Sierran morning shines
On summits rolling out like waves,
By many a brow of royal pines
The noisiest find quiet graves.

By lust of flesh and lust of gold,
And depth of loins and hairy breadth
Of breast, and hands to take and hold,
And boastful scorn of pain and death,
And something more of manliness
Than tamer men, and growing shame
Of shameful things, and something less
Of final faith in sword and flame --

By many a battle fought for wrong,
And many a battle fought for right,
So have you grown august and strong,
Magnificent in all men's sight --
A voice for which the kings have ears,
A face the craftiest statesmen scan;
A mind to mould the after years,
And mint the destinies of man!

Red sins were yours: the avid greed
Of pirate fathers, smocked as Grace,

Sent Judas missioners to read
Christ's Word to many a feebler race --
False priests of Truth who made their tryst
At Mammon's shrine, and reft or slew --
Some hands you taught to pray to Christ
Have prayed His curse to rest on you!

Your way has been to pluck the blade
Too readily, and train the guns.
We here, apart and unafraid
Of envious foes, are but your sons:
We stretched a heedless hand to smutch
Our spotless flag with Murder's blight --
For one less sacrilegious touch
God's vengeance blasted Uzza white!

You vaunted most of forts and fleets,
And courage proved in battle-feasts,
The courage of the beast that eats
His torn and quivering fellow-beasts;
Your pride of deadliest armament --
What is it but the self-same dint
Of joy with which the Caveman bent
To shape a bloodier axe of flint?

But praise to you, and more than praise
And thankfulness, for some things done;
And blessedness, and length of days
As long as earth shall last, or sun!
You first among the peoples spoke
Sharp words and angry questionings
Which burst the bonds and shed the yoke
That made your men the slaves of Kings!

You set and showed the whole world's school
The lesson it will surely read,
That each one ruled has right to rule --
The alphabet of Freedom's creed
Which slowly wins it proselytes
And makes uneasier many a throne;
You taught them all to prate of Rights
In language growing like your own!

And now your holiest and best
And wisest dream of such a tie
As, holding hearts from East to West,
Shall strengthen while the years go by:
And of a time when every man
For every fellow-man will do
His kindliest, working by the plan
God set him. May the dream come true!

And greater dreams! O Englishmen,
Be sure the safest time of all
For even the mightiest State is when
Not even the least desires its fall!
Make England stand supreme for aye,
Because supreme for peace and good,
Warned well by wrecks of yesterday
That strongest feet may slip in blood!

BARCROFT BOAKE

Barcroft Henry Thomas Boake was an Australian poet. Born in Sydney, Boake worked as a surveyor and a boundary rider but is best remembered for his poetry, a volume published five years after his death. His poems were all published posthumously in 1897 by A.G. Stephens in a collection titled "Where the Dead Men Lie: and Other Poems." "Where the Dead Men Lie" was the most famous of his poems, which described the tragedies Australians faced during the 1891–93 depression.

WHERE THE DEAD MEN LIE

Out on the wastes of the Never Never -
That's where the dead men lie!
There where the heat-waves dance forever -
That's where the dead men lie!
That's where the Earth's loved sons are keeping
Endless tryst: not the west wind sweeping
Feverish pinions can wake their sleeping -
Out where the dead men lie!

Where brown Summer and Death have mated -
That's where the dead men lie!
Loving with fiery lust unsated -
That's where the dead men lie!
Out where the grinning skulls bleach whitely
Under the saltbush sparkling brightly;
Out where the wild dogs chorus nightly -
That's where the dead men lie!

Deep in the yellow, flowing river -
That's where the dead men lie!
Under the banks where the shadows quiver -
That's where the dead men he!
Where the platypus twists and doubles,
Leaving a train of tiny bubbles.
Rid at last of their earthly troubles -
That's where the dead men lie!

East and backward pale faces turning -
That's how the dead men lie!
Gaunt arms stretched with a voiceless yearning -
That's how the dead men lie!

Oft in the fragrant hush of nooning
Hearing again their mother's crooning,
Wrapt for aye in a dreamful swooning -
That's how the dead men lie!

Only the hand of Night can free them -
That's when the dead men fly!
Only the frightened cattle see them -
See the dead men go by!
Cloven hoofs beating out one measure,
Bidding the stockmen know no leisure -
That's when the dead men take their pleasure!
That's when the dead men fly!

Ask, too, the never-sleeping drover:
He sees the dead pass by;
Hearing them call to their friends - the plover,
Hearing the dead men cry;
Seeing their faces stealing, stealing,
Hearing their laughter, pealing, pealing,
Watching their grey forms wheeling, wheeling
Round where the cattle lie!

Strangled by thirst and fierce privation -
That's how the dead men die!
Out on Moncygrub's farthest station -
That's how the dead men die!
Hard-faced greybeards, youngsters caflow;
Some mounds cared for, some left fallow;
Some deep down, yet others shallow.
Some having but the sky.

Moncygrub, as he sips his claret,
Looks with complacent eye
Down at his watch-chain, eighteen carat -
There, in his club, hard by:
Recks not that every link is stamped with
Names of the men whose limbs are cramped with
Too long lying in grave-mould, cramped with
Death where the dead men lie.

JACK'S LAST MUSTER

The first flush of grey light, the herald of daylight,
Is dimly outlining the musterer's camp,
Where over the sleeping, the stealthily creeping
Breath of the morning lies chilly and damp,

As, blankets forsaking, 'twixt sleeping and waking,
The black-boys turn out to the manager's call;
Whose order, of course, is, "Be after the horses,
And take all sorts of care you unhobble them all."

Then, each with a bridle (provokingly idle)
They saunter away his commands to fulfil -
Where, cheerily chiming, the musical rhyming
From equine bell-ringers comes over the hill.

But now the dull dawning gives place to the morning,
The sun, springing up in a glorious flood
Of golden-shot fire, mounts higher and higher,
Till the crests of the sandhills are stained with his
blood.

Now the hobble-chains' jingling, with the thud of hoofs
mingling,
Though distant, sound near - the cool air is so still -
As, urged by their whooping, the horses come trooping
In front of the boys round the point of the hill.

What searching and rushing for bridles and brushing
Of saddle marks, tight'ning of breastplate and girth;
And what a strange jumble of laughter and grumble -
Some comrade's misfortune the subject of mirth.

I recollect well how that morning Jack Bell
Had an argument over the age of a mare,
That C O B gray one, the dam of that bay one
Which Brown the storekeeper calls the young Lady
Clare.

How Tomboy and Vanity caused much profanity,
Scamping away with their tales in the air,
Till after a chase, at a deuce of a pace,
They ran back in the mob and we collared them
there.

Then the laugh and the banter, as gaily we canter,
With a pause for the nags at a miniature lake,
Where the "yellowtop" catches the sunlight in patches,
And lies like a mirror of gold in our wake.

Oh! the rush and the rattle of fast-fleeing cattle,
Whose hoofs beat a mad rataplan on the earth;
Their hot headed flight in! Who would not delight in
The gallop that seems to hold all that life is worth.

And over the rolling plains, slowly patrolling
To the sound of the cattle's monotonous tramp,
Till we hear the sharp pealing of stockwhips,
revealing
The fact that our comrades have put on the camp.

From the spot where they're drafting the wind rises,
wafting
The dust, till it hides man and beast from our gaze,
Till, suddenly lifting and easterly drifting,

We catch a short glimpse of the scene through the
haze.

What a blending and blurring of swiftly recurring
Colour and movement, that pass on their way
An intricate weaving of sights and sounds, leaving
An eager desire to take part in the fray:

A dusty procession, in circling succession,
Of bullocks that bellow in impotent rage;
A bright panorama, a soul stirring drama,
The sky for its background, the earth for its stage.

How well I remember that twelfth of November,
When Jack and his little mare, Vanity, fell;
On the Diamantina there never was seen a
Pair who could cut out a beast half so well.

And yet in one second Death's finger had beckoned,
And horse and bold rider had answered the call
Brooking no hesitation, without preparation,
That sooner or later must come to us all.

Thrice a big curly horned Cobb bullock had scorned
To meekly acknowledge the ruling of fate;
Thrice Jack with a clout of his whip cut him out,
But each time the beast galloped back to his mate.

Once more, he came blund'ring along, with Jack
thund'ring
Beside him, his spurs in poor Vanity's flanks,
As, from some cause or other forsaking its mother,

A little white calf trotted out from the ranks.

'Twas useless, I knew it, yet I turned to pursue it;
At the same time, I gave a loud warning to Jack:
It was all unavailing, I saw him come sailing
Along as the weaner ran into his track.

Little Vanity tried to turn off on one side,
Then altered her mind and attempted to leap;
The pace was too fast, that jump was her last,
For she and her rider fell all in a heap.

I was quickly down kneeling beside him, and feeling
With tremulous hand for the throb of his heart.
"The mare - is she dead?" were the first words he
said,
As he suddenly opened his eyes with a start.

He spoke to the creature, his hand could just reach
her,
Gently caressing her lean Arab head;
She acknowledged his praising with eyes quickly
glazing,
A whinny, a struggle, and there she lay
dead.

I sat there and nursed his head, for we durst
Not remove him, we knew where he fell he would die.
As I watched his life flicker, his breath growing
thicker,
I'd have given the world to be able to cry.

Roughvoiced, sunburnt men, far away beyond ken
Of civilisation, our comrades, stood nigh,
All true hearted mourners, and sadly forlorn, as
He gave them a handshake and bade them goodbye.

In my loving embrace there he finished life's race,
And nobly and gamely that long course was run;
Though a man and a sinner he weighed out a winner,
And God, the Great Judge, will declare he has won.

THE DEMON SNOW-SHOES
(A LEGEND OF KIANDRA)

The snow lies deep on hill and dale,
In rocky gulch and grassy vale,
The tiny, trickling, tumbling falls
Are frozen 'twixt their rocky walls
That grey and brown look silent down
Upon Kiandra's shrouded town.

The Eucumbene itself lies dead,
Fast frozen in its narrow bed,
And distant sounds ring out quite near,
The crystal air is froze so clear,
While to and fro the people go
In silent swiftness o'er the snow.

And, like a mighty gallows-frame,
The derrick in the New Chum claim
Hangs over where, despite the cold,
Strong miners seek the hidden gold,
And stiff and blue, half-frozen through,
The fickle dame of Fortune woo.

Far out, along a snow capped range,
There rose a sound which echoed strange,
Where snow-emburthen'd branches hang,
And flashing icicles, there rang
A gay refrain, as towards the plain
Sped swiftly downward Carl the Dane.

His long, lithe snow-shoes sped along

In easy rhythm to his song;
Now slowly circling round the hill,
Now speeding downward with a will;
The crystals crash and blaze and flash
As o'er the frozen crust they dash.

Among the hills the first he shone
Of all who buckled snow-shoe on,
For though the mountain lads were fleet,
But one bold rival dare compete,
To veer and steer, devoid of fear,
Beside this strong-limbed mountaineer.

'Twas Davy Eccleston who dared
To cast the challenge: If Carl cared
On shoes to try their mutual pace,
Then let him enter for the race,
Which might be run by anyone -
A would-be champion. Carl said "Done."

But not alone in point of speed
They sought to gain an equal meed,
For in the narrow lists of love,
Dave Eccleston had cast the glove:
Though both had prayed, the blushing maid
As yet no preference betrayed.

But played them off, as women will,
One 'gainst the other one, until
A day when she was sorely pressed
To loving neither youth confessed,
But did exclaim - the wily dame,

"Who wins this race, I'll bear his name!"

These words were running through Carl's head
As o'er the frozen crust he sped,
But suddenly became aware
That not alone he travelled there,
He sudden spied, with swinging stride,
A stranger speeding by his side;

The breezes o'er each shoulder toss'd
His beard, bediamonded with frost,
His eyes flashed strangely, bushy browed.
His breath hung round him like a shroud.
He never spoke, nor silence broke,
But by the Dane sped stroke for stroke.

"Old man! I neither know your name,
Nor what you are, nor whence you came:
But this, if I but had your shoes
This championship I ne'er could lose.
To call them mine, those shoes divine,
I'll gladly pay should you incline.

The stranger merely bowed his head -
"The shoes are yours," he gruffly said;
"I change with you, though at a loss,
And in return I ask that cross
Which, while she sung, your mother hung
Around your neck when you were young."

Carl hesitated when he heard
The price, but not for long demurred,

And gave the cross; the shoes were laced
Upon his feet in trembling haste,
So long and light, smooth polished, bright.
His heart beat gladly at the sight.

Now, on the morning of the race,
Expectancy on every face,
They come the programme to fulfil
Upon the slope of Township Hill;
With silent feet the people meet,
While youths and maidens laughing greet.

High-piled the flashing snowdrifts lie,
And laugh to scorn the sun's dull eye.
That, glistening feebly, seems to say -
"When Summer comes you'll melt away:
You'll change your song when I grow strong,
I think so, though I may be wrong."

The pistol flashed, and off they went
Like lightning on the steep descent,
Resistlessly down-swooping, swift
O'er the smooth face of polished drift
The racers strain with might and main.
But in the lead flies Carl the Dane.

Behind him Davy did his best,
With hopeless eye and lip compressed:
Beat by a snow-shoe length at most,
They flash and pass the winning-post.
The maiden said, "I'll gladly wed
The youth who in this race has led."

But where was he? still speeding fast,
Over the frozen stream he pass'd,
They watched his flying form until
They lost it over Sawyer's Hill,
Nor saw it more, the people swore
The like they'd never seen before.

The way he scaled that steep ascent
Was quite against all precedent,
While others said he could but choose
To do it on those demon shoes;
They talked in vain, for Carl the Dane
Was never seen in flesh again.

But now the lonely diggers say
That sometimes at the close of day
They see a misty wraith flash by
With the faint echo of a cry,
It may be true; perhaps they do,
I doubt it much; but what say you?

AN ALLEGORY

The fight was over, and the battle won
A soldier, who beneath his chieftain's eye
Had done a might deed and done it well,
And done it as the world will have it done—
A stab, a curse, some quick play of the butt,
Two skulls cracked crosswise, but the colours saved—
Proud of his wounds, proud of the promised cross,
Turned to his rear-rank man, who on his gun
Leant heavily apart. 'Ho, friend!' he called,
'You did not fight then: were you left behind?
I saw you not.' The other turned and showed
A gapping, red-lipped wound upon his breast.
'Ah,' said he sadly, 'I was in the smoke!'
Threw up his arms, shivered, and fell and died.

A SONG

I've a kiss from a warmer lover
Than maiden earth can be:
She blew it up to the skies above her,
And now it has come to me;
From the far-away it has come today
With a breath of the old salt sea.

She lay and laughed on a lazy billow,
Far away on the deep,
Who had gathered the froth for my lady's pillow -
Gathered a sparkling heap;
And the ocean's cry was the lullaby
That cradled my love to sleep.

Far away on the blue Pacific
There doth my lady roam,
That is oft-times gay, but as oft terrific:
Her jewels are beads of foam:
In a coral cave, where a blue-green wave
Keeps guard, is my lady's home.

She claps her hands, and her henchman hurries
West of the sunset sheen:
'Tis he who comes when a mist-wrack scurries,
Skirting the deep ravine;
And my heart is stirred by the loving word
He carries me from my queen.

A drop distilled from a lotos flower -
That is the magic key
To unlock the cage, and my soul has power

To gather itself and flee,
At my love's behest, where she waits her guest
In a palace beneath the sea.

Joy is ours that is almost anguish:
Pain that is almost sweet:
We kiss; and the ocean creatures languish
Jealously at our feet;
The sight grows dim, and the senses swim
When I and my lady greet.

There to dream, while the soul is swooning
Under a woven spell -
Hushed to sleep by her tender crooning
Learnt from the ocean swell -
There to rest on her jewelled breast,
To love and be loved as well!

VICTOR DALEY

Victor James William Patrick Daley was an Irish-born Australian poet. Daley serves chiefly as an example of the Celtic Twilight in Australian verse. He also serves as a lyrical alternative to his contemporary bush balladists Henry Lawson, Banjo Paterson, and Will H. Ogilvie. His ambition was to earn a living purely as a writer, which was, at the time, unusual. His work was not considered mainly Australian but quite lyrical, with 'natural delicacy of expression, graceful imagery, and refinement of language.' His Poems (1908) and other collections were published posthumously. Daley's finest Australian work was considered to be A Sunset Fantasy.

A SUNSET FANTASY

Spellbound by a sweet fantasy
At evenglow I stand
Beside an opaline strange sea
That rings a sunset land.
The rich lights fade out one by one,
And, like a peony
Drowning in wine, the crimson sun
Sinks down in that strange sea.

His wake across the ocean-floor
In a long glory lies,
Like a gold wave-way to the shore
Of some sea paradise.

My dream flies after him, and I
Am in another land;
The sun sets in another sky,
And we sit hand in hand.

Gray eyes look into mine; such eyes
I think the angel's are—
Soft as the soft light in the skies
When shines the morning star,

And tremulous as morn, when thin
Gold lights begin to glow,
Revealing the bright soul within
As dawn the sun below.

So, hand in hand, we watch the sun
Burn down the Western deeps,

Dreaming a charmed dream, as one
Who in enchantment sleeps;

A dream of how we twain some day,
Careless of map or chart,
Will both take ship and sail away
Into the sunset's heart.

Our ship shall be of sandal built,
Like ships in old-world tales,
Carven with cunning art, and gilt,
And winged with scented sails

Of silver silk, whereon the red
Great gladioli burn,
A rainbow-flag at her masthead,
A rose-flag at her stern;

And, perching on the point above
Wherefrom the pennon blows,
The figure of a flying dove,
And in her beak a rose.

And from the fading land the breeze
Shall bring us, blowing low,
Old odours and old memories,
And airs of long ago—

A melody that has no words
Of mortal speech a part,
Yet touching all the deepest chords
That tremble in the heart:

A scented song blown oversea,
As though from bowers of bloom
A wind-harp in a lilac-tree
Breathed music and perfume.

And we, no more with longings pale,
Will smile to hear it blow;
I in the shadow of the sail,
You in the sunset-glow.

For, with the fading land, our fond
Old fears shall all fade out,
Paled by the light from shores beyond
The dread of Death or Doubt.

And from a gloomy cloud above
When Death his shadow flings,
The Spirit of Immortal Love
Will shield us with his wings.

He is the lord of dreams divine,
And lures us with his smiles
Along the splendour opaline
Unto the Blessed Isles.

SONG

What shall a man remember
In days when he is old,
And Life is a dying ember,
And Fame a story told?

Power—that came to leave him?
Wealth—to the wild waves blown?
Fame—that came to deceive him?
Ah, no! Sweet Love alone!

Honour, and Wealth, and Power
May all like dreams depart—
But Love is a fadeless flower
Whose roots are in the heart.

LOVE

Love is the sunlight of the soul,
That, shining on the silken-tressèd head
Of her we love, around it seems to shed
A golden angel-aureole.

And all her ways seem sweeter ways
Than those of other women in that light:
She has no portion with the pallid night,
But is a part of all fair days.

Joy goes where she goes, and good dreams—
Her smile is tender as an old romance
Of Love that dies not, and her soft eye's glance
Like sunshine set to music seems.

Queen of our fate is she, but crowned
With purple hearts-ease for her womanhood.
There is no place so poor where she has stood
But evermore is holy ground.

An angel from the heaven above
Would not be fair to us as she is fair:
She holds us in a mesh of silken hair,
This one sweet woman whom we love.

We pray thee, Love, our souls to steep
In dreams wherein thy myrtle flowereth;
So when the rose leaves shiver, feeling Death
Pass by, we may remain asleep:

Asleep, with poppies in our hands,
From all the world and all its cares apart—
Cheek close to cheek, heart beating against heart,
While through Life's sandglass run the sands

'UNTO THIS LAST'

They brought my fair love out upon a bier—
Out from the dwelling that her smile made sweet,
Out from the life that her life made complete,
Into the glitter of the garish street—
And no man wept, save I, for that dead dear.
And then the dark procession wound along,
Like a black serpent with a snow-white bird
Held in its fangs. I think God said a word
To death, as He in His chill heaven heard
Her voice so sweeter than His seraph's song.

And so Death took away her flower-sweet breath
One darkest day of days in a dark year,
And brought to that strong God who had no fear
My own dear love. Ah, closed eyes without peer!
Ah, red lips pressed on the blue lips of Death!

A PICTURE

The Sun burns fiercely down the skies;
The sea is full of flashing eyes;
The waves glide shoreward serpentwise
And fawn with foamy tongues on stark
Gray rocks, each sharp-toothed as a shark,
And hiss in clefts and channels dark.

Blood-purple soon the waters grow,
As though drowned sea-kings fought below
Forgotten fights of long ago.

The gray owl Dusk its wings has spread;
The sun sinks in a blossom-bed
Of poppy-clouds; the day is dead.

CHRISTMAS IN AUSTRALIA

O DAY, the crown and crest of all the year!

Thou comest not to us amid the snows,

But midmost of the reign of the red rose;

Our hearts have not yet lost the ancient cheer

That filled our fathers' simple hearts when 'ere

The leaves fell, and the winds of Winter froze

The waters wan, and carols at the close

Of yester-eve sang the Child Christ anear.

And so we hail thee with a greeting high,

And drain to thee a draught of our own wine,

Forgetful not beneath this bluer sky

Of that old mother-land beyond the brine,

Whose gray skies gladden as thou drawest nigh,

O day of God's good-will the seal and sign!

HIS SOUL

ONCE from the world of living men
I passed, by a strange fancy led,
To a still City of the Dead,
To call upon a citizen.

He had been famous in his day;
Much talked of, written of, and praised
For virtues my small soul amazed—
And yet I thought his heart was clay.

He was too full of grace for me:
His friends said, on a marble stone,
His soul sat somewhere near the Throne
I did not know; I called to see.

His name and fame were on the door—
A most superior tomb indeed,
Much railed, and gilt, and filigreed;
He occupied the lower floor.

I knocked—a worm crawled from its hole:
I looked—and knew it for his soul.

A VISION OF YOUTH

A horseman on a hilltop green
Drew rein, and wound his horn;
So bright he looked he might have been
The Herald of the Morn.
His steed was of the sovran strain
In Fancy's meadows bred—
And pride was in his tossing mane,
And triumph in his tread.

The rider's eyes like jewels glowed—
The World was in his hand—
As down the woodland way he rode
When Spring was in the land.

From golden hour to golden hour
For him the woodland sang.
And from the heart of every flower
A singing fairy sprang.

He rode along with rein so free,
And, as he rode, the Blue
Mysterious Bird of Fantasy
Ever before him flew.

He rode by cot and castle dim
Through all the greenland gay;
Bright eyes through casements glanced at him:
He laughed—and rode away.

The world with sunshine was aflood,
And glad were maid and man,

And through his throbbing veins the blood
In keen, sweet shudders ran.

His steed tossed head with fiery scorn,
And stamped, and snuffed the air—
As though he heard a sudden horn
Of far-off battle blare.
Erect the rider sat awhile
With flashing eyes, and then
Turned slowly, sighing, with a smile,
"O weary world of men!"

For aye the Bird of Fantasy
Sang magic songs to him,
And deeper and deeper still rode he
Into the Forest Dim.

That rider with his face aglow
With joy of life I see
In dreams. Ah, years and years ago
He parted ways with me!
Yet, sometimes, when the days are drear
And all the world forlorn,
From out the dim wood's heart I hear
The echo of his horn.

DISILLUSION

For some forty years, and over,
Poets had with me their way;
And they made me think that Sorrow
Owned the Night and owned the Day;
And the corpse beneath the clover
Had a hopeful word to say.

And they made me think that Sorrow
Was the Shadow in the Sun;
And they made me think To-morrow
Was a gift to everyone:
And the days I used to borrow,
Till my credit now is done.

And they told me softly, sweetly,
That, when Life had lost its glee,
I could be consoled completely

By the Forest or the Sea;
And they wrote their rhymes so neatly
That they quite deluded me.

But when Sorrow is at sorest,
And the heart weeps silently,
Is there healing in the Forest?
Is there solace in the Sea?
And the God whom thou adorest
Has He any help for thee?

Does it soothe the spent man dying
That the stars are shining bright

O'er the field where he is lying?
And the moon, with all her light,
Does she help his bare soul flying
Through the vast and lonely Night?

Give to me the grasp of true man,
Though his state be high or low,
Give to me the kiss of woman—
Let your Seas and Forests go:
There is nothing but the human
Touch can heal the human woe.

MYRA MORRIS

Myra Morris was an Australian poet, novelist, and writer for children. Morris began publishing poetry and short stories in various Australian newspapers and magazines in her early twenties, and her first volume of poetry, England and Other Verses, appeared in 1918. Morris wrote for many newspapers and periodicals and was active in founding and organizing the Melbourne branch of P.E.N. International. She often portrayed the joyful lifting of the spirits that a person could feel from a simple walk in the country.

A MORNING WALK

From Frankston into Cranbourne
The road runs all along
Between green-golden stretches,
A lovely way of song,
With thrushes singing loud and gay
And blackbirds clear and strong.
From Frankston into Cranbourne
We went, and cared for none.

The pines along the wayside
Showed yellow shoots, each one;
And the bare old orchard trees were gray
As cobwebs in the sun.
Where the bracken's frosted silver
Rimmed spikes of pearly heath
We saw the cream clematis
Weave lacy wreath on wreath
Above the jade-green fuchsia bells
And greenhoods underneath.

The purple sarsparilla
Spread out a cloak of pride,
And flat-faced little sundews——
Each chalice opened wide——
Were white flotillas floating on
Some tangled, moveless tide.
We knelt beside still waters,
As dark as dark could be,
And plucked the strange swamp-lilies,
Their fretted ivory
Flung up in two black-dusted wings
With fairy symmetry.
We watched the firesmoke rising

Behind its dim blue veil;
The shy young gum-trees dancing
In a vision sweet and frail,
And the far-off hills that lay in dream,
Pale as the dawn is pale.

From Frankston into Cranbourne
The road runs all along
Between green-golden stretches,
The lovely way of song,
With thrushes singing loud and gay
And blackbirds clear and strong.

MARCUS CLARKE

Marcus Andrew Hislop Clarke was an English-born Australian novelist, journalist, poet, editor, librarian, and playwright. He is best known for his 1874 novel For the Term of His Natural Life, about Australia's convict system, and is widely regarded as a classic of Australian literature. It has been adapted into many plays, films, and folk operas. Clarke was an important literary figure in Australia and at the center of a bohemian circle in Melbourne. He was inducted into The Australian Media Hall of Fame in 2017.

THE SONG OF TIGILAU

The song of Tigilau the brave,
Sina's wild lover,
Who across the heaving wave
From Samoa came over:
Came over, Sina, at the setting moon!

The moon shines round and bright;
She, with her dark-eyed maidens at her side,
Watches the rising tide.
While balmy breathes the starry southern night,
While languid heaves the lazy southern tide;
The rising tide, O Sina, and the setting moon!

The night is past, is past and gone,
The moon sinks to the West,
The sea-heart beats opprest,
And Sina's passionate breast
Heaves like the sea, when the pale moon has gone,
Heaves like the passionate sea, Sina, left by the moon alone!

Silver on silver sands, the rippling waters meet —
Will he come soon?
The rippling waters kiss her delicate feet,
The rippling waters, lisping low and sweet,
Ripple with the tide,
The rising tide,
The rising tide, O Sina, and the setting moon!

He comes! — her lover!
Tigilau, the son of Tui Viti.
Her maidens round her hover,

The rising waves her white feet cover.

O Tigilau, son of Tui Viti,

Through the mellow dusk thy proas glide,

So soon!

So soon by the rising tide,

The rising tide, my Sina, and the setting moon!

The mooring-poles are left,

The whitening waves are cleft,

By the prows of Tui Viti!

By the sharp keels of Tui Viti!

Broad is the sea, and deep,

The yellow Samoans sleep,

But they will wake and weep —

Weep in their luxurious odorous vales,

While the land breeze swells the sails

Of Tui Viti!

Tui Viti — far upon the rising tide,

The rising tide —

The rising tide, my Sina, beneath the setting moon!

She leaps to meet him!

Her mouth to greet him

Burns at his own.

Away! To the canoes,

To the yoked war canoes!

The sea in murmurous tone

Whispers the story of their loves,

Re-echoes the story of their loves —

The story of Tui Viti,

Of Sina and Tui Viti,

By the rising tide,

The rising tide, Sina, beneath the setting moon!

She has gone!
She has fled!
Sina!
Sina, for whom the warriors decked their shining hair,
Wreathing with pearls their bosoms brown and bare,
Flinging beneath her dainty feet
Mats crimson with the feathers of the parakeet.
Ho, Samoans! rouse your warriors full soon,
For Sina is across the rippling wave,
With Tigilau, the bold and brave.
Far, far upon the rising tide!
Far upon the rising tide!
Far upon the rising tide, Sina, beneath the setting moon.

IN A LADY'S ALBUM

WHAT can I write in thee, O dainty book,
About whose daintiness faint perfume lingers—
Into whose pages dainty ladies look,
And turn thy dainty leaves with daintier fingers?

Fitter my ruder muse for ruder song,
My scrawling quill to coarser paper matches;
My voice, in laughter raised too loud and long,
Is hoarse and cracked with singing tavern catches.

No melodies have I for ladies' ear,
No roundelays for jocund lads and lasses—
But only brawlings born of bitter beer,
And chorussed with the clink and clash of glasses!

So, tell thy mistress, pretty friend, for me,
I cannot do her hest, for all her frowning,
While dust and ink are but polluting thee,
And vile tobacco-smoke thy leaves embrowning.

Thou breathest purity and humble worth—
The simple jest, the light laugh following after.
I will not jar upon thy modest mirth
With harsher jest, or with less gentle laughter.

So, some poor tavern-haunter, steeped in wine,
With staggering footsteps thro' the streets returning,
Seeing, through gathering glooms, a sweet light shine
From household lamp in happy window burning,

May pause an instant in the wind and rain
To gaze on that sweet scene of love and duty,
But turns into the wild wet night again,
Lest his sad presence mar its holy beauty.

AN AUSTRALIAN PAEAN—1876

The English air is fresh and fair,
The Irish fields are green;
The bright light gleams o'er Scotland's streams,
And glows her hills between.
The hawthorn is in blossom,
And birds from every bough
Make musical the dewy spring
In April England now.

Our April bears no blossoms,
No promises of spring;
Her gifts are rain and storm and stain,
And surges lash and swing.
No budded wreath doth she bequeath,
Her tempests toss the trees;
No balmy gales—but shivered sails,
And desolated seas.

Yet still we love our April,
For it aids us to bequeath
A gift more fair than blossoms rare,
More sweet than budded wreath.
Our children's tend'rest memories
Round Austral April grow;
'Twas the month we won their freedom, boys,
Just twenty years ago.

Though Scotland has her forests,
Though Erin has her vales,
Though plentiful her harvests,
In England's sunny dales;

Yet foul amidst the fairness,
The factory chimneys smoke,
And the murmurs of the many
In their burdened bosoms choke.

We hear the children's voices
'Mid the rattle of its looms,
Crying, "Wherefore shut God's heaven
All our golden afternoons?"
Though here the English April
Nor song nor sun imparts,
Its Spring is on our children's lips,
Its summer in their hearts!

We've left the land that bore us,
Its castles and its shrines;
We've changed the cornfields and the rye
For the olives and the vines.
Yet still we have our castles,
Yet still we bow the knee;
We each enshrine a saint divine,
And her name is Liberty.

Liberty! name of warning!
Did'st thou feel our pulses beat
As we marching, moved this morning
All adown the cheering street?
In our federated freedom,
In our manliness allied,
While the badges of our labour
Were the banners of our pride.

Did our fancies speak prophetic
Of a larger league than this—
With higher aims and nobler claims
To grasp the good we miss;
When in freer federation
In a future yet to be,
Australia stands a nation
From the centre to the sea.

Cheer for Australia, comrades,
And cheer for Britain, too;
Who loves them both will not be loth
To give each land its due.
So cheer for Britain, comrades;
Our fathers loved the soil,
And the grandeur of her greatness
Is the measure of their toil.

But never let our sons forget,
Till mem'ry's self be dead,
If Britain gave us birth, my lads,
Australia gave us bread!
Then cheer for young Australia,
The empire of the Free,
Where yet a Greater Britain
The Southern Cross shall see!

THE WAIL OF THE WAITER

All day long, at Scott's or Menzies', I await the gorging crowd,

Panting, penned within a pantry, with the blowflies humming loud,

There at seven in the morning do I count my daily cash,

While the home-returning reveller calls for 'soda and a dash'.

And the weary hansom-cabbies set the blinking squatters down,

Who, all night, in savage freedom, have been 'knocking round the town'.

Soon the breakfast gong resounding bids the festive meal begin,

And, with appetites like demons, come the gentle public in.

'Toast and butter!' 'Eggs and coffee!' 'Waiter, mutton cops for four!'

'Flatheads!' 'Ham!' 'Beef!' 'Where's the mustard?' 'Steak and onions!'
'Shut the door!'

Here sits bandicoot, the broker, eating in a desperate hurry,

Scowling at his left-hand neighbour, Cornstalk from the Upper Murray,

Who with brandy-nose enpurpled, and with blue lips cracked and dry,

In incipient delirium shoves the eggspoon in his eye.

'Bloater paste!' 'Some tender steak, sir?' 'Here, confound you, where's my
chop?'

'Waiter!' 'Yessir!' 'Waiter!' 'Yessir!!' - running till I'm fit to drop.

Then at lunch time -- fearful crisis! In by shoals the gorgers pour,

Gobbling, crunching, swilling, munching -- ten times hungrier than before.

'Glass of porter!' 'Ale for me, John!' 'Where's my stick?' 'And where's my
hat!'

'Oxtal soup!' 'I asked for curry!' 'Cold boiled beef, and cut it fat!'

'Irish stew!' 'Some pickled cabbage!' 'What, no beans?' 'Bring me some
pork!'

'Soup, sir?' 'Yes. You grinning idiot, can I eat it with a FORK?'

'Take care, waiter!' 'Beg your pardon.' 'Curse you, have you two left legs?'

'I asked for bread an hour ago, sir!' 'Now then, have you laid those eggs?'

'Sherry!' 'No, I called for beer -- of all the fools I ever saw!'

'Waiter!' 'Yessir!' 'WAITER!!' 'Here, sir!' 'Damme, sir, this steak is

RAW!'

Thus amid this hideous Babel do I live the livelong day,

While my memory is going, and my hair is turning grey.

All my soul is slowly melting, all my brain is softening fast,

And I know that I'll be taken to the Yarr bend at last.

For at night from fitful slumbers I awaken with a start,

Murmuring of steak and onions, babbling of apple-tart.

While to me the Poet's cloudland a gigantic kitchen seems,

And those mislaid table-napkins haunt me even in my dreams

Is this right? -- Ye sages tell me! -- Does a man live but to eat?

Is there nothing worth enjoying but one's miserable meat?

Is the mightiest task of genius but to swallow buttered beans,

And has man but been created to demolish pork and greens?

Is there no unfed Hereafter, where the round of chewing stops?

Is the atmosphere of heaven clammy with perpetual chops?

Do the friends of Mr Naylor sup on spirit-reared cow-heel?

Can the great Alexis Soyer really say 'Soyez tranquille?'

Or must I bring spirit beefsteak grilled in spirit regions hotter

For the spirit delectation of some spiritual squatter?

Shall I in a spirit kitchen hear the spirit blowflies humming,

Calming spiritual stomachs with a spiritual 'Coming!'?

Shall -- but this is idle chatter, I have got my work to do.

'WAITER!!' 'Yessir.' 'Wake up, stupid! Boiled calves' feet for Number
Two!'

EDWARD DYSON

Edward George Dyson (4 March 1865 – 22 August 1931), or 'Ted' Dyson, was an Australian journalist, poet, playwright, and short story writer. Dyson wrote under several – some say many – noms-de-plume, including Silas Snell. He was a great observer of life around him, though, being more or less at liberty to explore wherever he chose. There were a lot of disused gold mines near his home. These were a source of constant wonder and excitement, along with the characters he found in the town. Many of them were remembered in his future stories of miners and mining. One of his childhood haunts, a town called Alfredton, became "Waddy" in his stories and poems. His experiences in the gold fields were a rich source of material, but he also wrote about other industrial processes.

THE OLD WHIM HORSE

He's an old grey horse, with his head bowed sadly,
And with dim old eyes and a queer roll aft,
With the off-fore sprung and the hind screwed badly,
And he bears all over the brands of graft;
And he lifts his head from the grass to wonder
Why by night and day the whim is still,
Why the silence is, and the stampers' thunder
Sounds forth no more from the shattered mill.
In that whim he worked when the night winds bellowed
On the riven summit of Giant's Hand,
And by day when prodigal Spring had yellowed
All the wide, long sweep of enchanted land;
And he knew his shift, and the whistle's warning,
And he knew the calls of the boys below;
Through the years, unbidden, at night or morning,
He had taken his stand by the old whim bow.

But the whim stands still, and the wheeling swallow
In the silent shaft hangs her home of clay,
And the lizards flirt and the swift snakes follow
O'er the grass-grown brace in the summer day;
And the corn springs high in the cracks and corners
Of the forge, and down where the timber lies;
And the crows are perched like a band of mourners
On the broken hut on the Hermit's Rise.

All the hands have gone, for the rich reef paid out,
And the company waits till the calls come in;
But the old grey horse, like the claim, is played out,
And no market's near for his bones and skin.
So they let him live, and they left him grazing

By the creek, and oft in the evening dim
I have seen him stand on the rises, gazing
At the ruined brace and the rotting whim.

The floods rush high in the gully under,
And the lightnings lash at the shrinking trees,
Or the cattle down from the ranges blunder
As the fires drive by on the summer breeze.
Still the feeble horse at the right hour wanders
To the lonely ring, though the whistle's dumb,
And with hanging head by the bow he ponders
Where the whim boy's gone—why the shifts don't come.

But there comes a night when he sees lights glowing
In the roofless huts and the ravaged mill,
When he hears again all the stampers going—
Though the huts are dark and the stampers still:
When he sees the steam to the black roof clinging
As its shadows roll on the silver sands,
And he knows the voice of his driver singing,
And the knocker's clang where the braceman stands.

See the old horse take, like a creature dreaming,
On the ring once more his accustomed place;
But the moonbeams full on the ruins streaming
Show the scattered timbers and grass-grown brace.
Yet he hears the sled in the smithy falling,
And the empty truck as it rattles back,
And the boy who stands by the anvil, calling;
And he turns and backs, and he "takes up slack".

While the old drum creaks, and the shadows shiver

As the wind sweeps by, and the hut doors close,
    And the bats dip down in the shaft or quiver
In the ghostly light, round the grey horse goes;
And he feels the strain on his untouched shoulder,
    Hears again the voice that was dear to him,
Sees the form he knew—and his heart grows bolder
    As he works his shift by the broken whim.

He hears in the sluices the water rushing
    As the buckets drain and the doors fall back;
When the early dawn in the east is blushing,
    He is limping still round the old, old track.
Now he pricks his ears, with a neigh replying
    To a call unspoken, with eyes aglow,
And he sways and sinks in the circle, dying;
    From the ring no more will the grey horse go.

In a gully green, where a dam lies gleaming,
    And the bush creeps back on a worked-out claim,
And the sleepy crows in the sun sit dreaming
    On the timbers grey and a charred hut frame,
Where the legs slant down, and the hare is squatting
    In the high rank grass by the dried-up course,
Nigh a shattered drum and a king-post rotting
    Are the bleaching bones of the old grey horse.

AN INEQUITABLE IMPOST

The first one with conviction penned:
"This conflict in seven weeks will end."

Another, later in the war,
Gave Germany just one month more.

Since then I've read predictions free –
They dribble in unceasingly.

All wrong. And still the critics say
When it will finish to the day.

Hughes should get cash in mighty sacks
From his proposed War Prophets Tax.

MY TYPEWRITER

I have a trim typewriter now,
They tell me none is better;
It makes a pleasing, rhythmic row,
And neat is every letter.
I tick out stories by machine,
Dig pars, and gags, and verses keen,
And lathe them off in manner slick.
It is so easy, and it's quick.

And yet it falls short, I'm afraid,
Of giving satisfaction,
This making literature by aid
Of scientific traction;
For often, I can't fail to see,
The dashed thing runs away with me.
It bolts, and do whate'er I may
I cannot hold the runaway.

It is not fitted with a brake,
And endless are my verses,
Nor any yarn I start to make
Appropriately terse is.
'Tis plain that this machine-made screed
Is fit but for machines to read;
So "Wanted" (as an iron censor)
"A good, sound, secondhand condenser!"

CRICKET IS A SERIOUS THING

In politics there's room for jest;
With frequent gibes are speeches met,
And measures which are of the best
Are themes for caustic humor yet.
E'en though the pulpiteer we fret
With sundry quiddities we fling,
We pray you never to forget
That cricket is a serious thing.

The crowd assembles at a Test,
And Hobbs at length is fairly set,
Though Gregory rocks 'em in with zest;
The barrackers may fume and fret
When Parkin has contrived to get
Five men of ours – we feel the sting,
And give expression to regret,
For cricket is a serious thing.

They have the lead; we would arrest
A sort of rot.No epithet
Is proper, though they've got our best
For next to nothing, and your bet
Is good as lost.Don't sit and sweat;
Due reverence to the problem bring.
We have a pile of runs to net –
Ah, cricket is a serious thing.

THE FACT OF THE MATTER

I'm wonderin' why those fellers who go buildin' chipper ditties,
'Bout the rosy times out drovin', an' the dust an' death of cities,
Don't sling the bloomin' office, strike some drover for a billet,
And soak up all the glory that comes handy while they fill it.

P'r'aps it's fun to travel cattle or to picnic with merinos,
But the drover don't catch on, sir, not much high-class rapture he knows.
As for sleepin' on the plains there in the shadder of the spear-grass,
That's liked best by the Juggins with a spring-bed an' a pier-glass.

An' the camp-fire, an' the freedom, and the blanky constellations,
The 'possum-rug an' billy, an' the togs an' stale ole rations,
It's strange they're only raved about by coves that dress up pretty,
An' sport a wife, an' live on slap-up tucker in the city.

I've tickled beef in my time clear from Clarke to Riverina,
An' shifted sheep all round the shop, but blow me if I've seen a
Single blanky hand who didn't buck at pleasures of this kidney,
And wouldn't trade his blisses for a flutter down in Sydney.

Night-watches are delightful when the stars are really splendid
To the chap who's fresh upon the job, but, you bet, his rapture's ended
When the rain comes down in sluice-heads, or the cuttin' hailstones pelter,
An' the sheep drift off before the wind, an' the horses strike for shelter.

Don't take me for a howler, but I find it come annoyin'
To hear these fellers rave about the pleasures we're enjoyin',
When p'r'aps we've nothin' better than some fluky water handy,
An' they're right on all the lickers, rum, an' plenty beer an' brandy.

The town is dusty, may be, but it isn't worth the curses

'Side the dust a feller swallers an' the blinded thirst he nurses
When he's on the hard macadam, where the jumbucks cannot browse, an'
The wind is in his whiskers, an' he follers twenty thousan'.

This drovin' on the plain, too, it's all O.K. when the weather
Isn't hot enough to curl the soles right off your upper leather,
Or so cold that when the mornin' wind comes hissin' through the grasses
You can feel it cut your eyelids like a whip-lash as it passes.

Then there's bull-ants in the blankets, an' a lame horse, an' muskeeters,
An' a D.T. boss like Halligan, or one like Humpy Peters,
Who is mean about the tucker, an' can curse from start to sundown,
An' can fight like fifty devils, an' whose growler's never run down.

Yes, I wonder why the fellers what go building chipper ditties
'Bout the rosy times out drovin' an' the dust an' death of cities,
Don't sling the bloomin' office, strike ole Peters for a billet,
An' soak up all the glory that comes handy while they fill it.

QUITS

Ben Unger's wife was dark and small,
With little, round, black eyes;
Ben Unger started at her call,
For Ben had been made wise.
No dirge could crush his spirit but
The one by Annie sung;
No whip-lash ever made could cut
Like Annie Unger's tongue.

But Annie had a round, red cheek,
A figure like a plum,
And Henderson from up the creek
In courtship sly would come.
Then Annie voiced no angry call,
Here dirge remained unsung,
And very gentle was the fall
Of Annie Unger's tongue.

Ned Holman went to Ben upon
The hill in Colter's hay.
He said: "your wife with Henderson
Ran off at ten to-day!"
Ben stood stock still. "All right!" said he;
Then with a little laugh:
"That makes us quits at last. 'Twas me
That stole his brindle calf!"

BULLOCKY BILL

FROM a river siding, the railway town,
Or the dull new port there three days down,
Forward and back on the up-hill track,
With a creak of the jinker, a ringing crack,
Slow as a funeral, sure as steam,
Bullocky Bill and his old red team.

Ploughing around by the ti-tree scrub,
Four wheels down to the creeping hub,
Swaying they go, with their heads all low,
Bally, and Splodger, and Spot, and Jo.
Men in the ranges much esteem
Bullocky Bill and his old red team.

Worming about where the tall trees spring,
Surging ahead when the clay bogs cling;
A rattle of lash and of language rash
On the narrow edge of immortal smash.
He'd thread a bead or walk a beam,
Bullocky Bill with his old red team.

Climbing a ridge where the red stars ride;
Straddling down on the other side,
With a whistle and grind, and a scramble blind,
And a thundering gum-tree slung behind.
But they always get there, hill or stream,
Bullocky Bill and his old red team.

Engines or stamps for the mines about,
Tools for the men who are leading out;
Tucker, and boose, and the latest news
Back where the bunyip stirs the ooze.
Pioneers with the best we deem
Bullocky Bill and his old red team.

AS THE TROOPS WENT THROUGH

I heard this day, as I may no more,
The world's heart throb at my workshop door.
The sun was keen, and the day was still;
The township drowsed in, a haze of heat.
A stir far off on the sleepy hill,
The measured beat of their buoyant feet,
And the lilt and thrum
Of a little drum,
The song they sang in a cadence low,
The piping note of a piccolo.

The township woke, and the doors flew wide;
The women trotted their boys beside.
Across the bridge on a single heel
The soldiers came in a golden glow,
With throb of song and the chink of steel,
The gallant crow of the piccolo.
Good and brown they were,
And their arms swung bare.
Their fine young faces revived in me
A boyhood's vision of chivalry.

The lean, hard regiment tramping down,
Bushies, miners and boys from town.
From 'mid the watchers the road along
One fell in line with the khaki men.
He took the stride, and he caught their song,
And Steve went then, and Meneer, and Ben,
Long Dave McCree,
And the Weavers three,
All whisked away by the "Come! Come! Come!"

The lusty surge of the vaunting drum.

I swore a prayer for each soldier lad.
He was the son that might have had;
The tall, bold boy who was never mine,
All brave with dust that the eyes laughed through,
His shoulders square, and his chin in line,
Was marching too with the gallant few.
Passed the muffled beat
Of their swanking feet,
The swell of drum, the exulting crow,
The wild-bird note of the piccolo.

They dipped away in the listless trees;
A mother wept on her beaded knees
For sons gone out to the long war's end;
But more than mother or man wept I
Who had no son in the world to send.
The hour lagged by, and drifting high
Came the fitful hum
Of the little drum,
And faint, but still with an ardent flow,
The pibroch, call of the piccolo.

THE AUCTION

"Who'll bid?Who'll bid?" the question rang
Where throned Death was calling.
I seemed to sense his charnel tang,
Mephitic air appalling;
And every tick I heard the clang
Of his steel hammer falling.

Come great men who upon our earth
Had held a lofty mission,
The spacious ones of lordly birth,
The cunning politician,
And gentlemen of holy worth
Or wondrous erudition.

One buyer in a corner trolls
Beyond the ghastly revel.
He buys by lots or single souls,
His voice is low and level.
And paltry is the price he doles.
The buyer is the Devil!

C. J. DENNIS

Clarence Michael James Stanislaus Dennis, better known as C. J. Dennis, was an Australian poet and journalist for his best-selling verse novel The Songs of a Sentimental Bloke. Alongside his contemporaries and occasional collaborators Henry Lawson and Banjo Paterson, Dennis helped popularise Australian slang in literature, earning him the title 'the laureate of the larrikin.' Still regarded as one of Australia's literary masterpieces, in its day, the "Sentimental Bloke" broke all publishing records in this country and overseas. Just as important was the timing of the publication; it reached a public depressed by enormous war casualties. It had phenomenal success because of the broad appeal of sentiment and humor in its simple love story.

THE SWAGMAN

Oh, he was old and he was spare;
His bushy whiskers and his hair
Were all fussed up and very grey
He said he'd come a long, long way
And had a long, long way to go.
Each boot was broken at the toe,
And he'd a swag upon his back.
His billy-can, as black as black,
Was just the thing for making tea
At picnics, so it seemed to me.

'Twas hard to earn a bite of bread,
He told me.Then he shook his head,
And all the little corks that hung
Around his hat-brim danced and swung
And bobbed about his face; and when
I laughed he made them dance again.
He said they were for keeping flies -
"The pesky varmints" - from his eyes.
He called me "Codger". . . "Now you see
The best days of your life," said he.
"But days will come to bend your back,
And, when they come, keep off the track.
Keep off, young codger, if you can.
He seemed a funny sort of man.

He told me that he wanted work,
But jobs were scarce this side of Bourke,
And he supposed he'd have to go
Another fifty mile or so.
"Nigh all my life the track I've walked,"

He said.I liked the way he talked.

And oh, the places he had seen!

I don't know where he had not been -

On every road, in every town,

All through the country, up and down.

"Young codger, shun the track," he said.

And put his hand upon my head.

I noticed, then, that his old eyes

Were very blue and very wise.

"Ay, once I was a little lad,"

He said, and seemed to grow quite sad.

I sometimes think: When I'm a man,

I'll get a good black billy-can

And hang some corks around my hat,

And lead a jolly life like that.

The Austra——laise

Fellers of Australier,

Blokes an' coves an' coots,

Shift yer —— carcases,

Move yer —— boots.

Gird yer —— loins up,

Get yer —— gun,

Set the —— enermy

An' watch the —— run.

Chorus:

Get a —— move on,

Have some —— sense.

Learn the —— art of
Self de- —— -fence.
Have some —— brains be-
Neath yer —— lids.
An' swing a —— sabre
Fer the missus an' the kids.
Chuck supportin' —— posts,
An' strikin' —— lights,
Support a —— fam'ly an'
Strike fer yer —— rights.

Chorus:
Get a —— move, etc.
Joy is —— fleetin',
Life is —— short.
Wot's the use uv wastin' it
All on —— sport?
Hitch yer —— tip-dray
To a —— star.
Let yer —— watchword be
"Australi- —— -ar!"

Chorus:
Get a —— move, etc.
'Ow's the —— nation
Goin' to ixpand
'Lest us —— blokes an' coves
Lend a —— 'and?
'Eave yer —— apathy
Down a —— chasm;
'Ump yer —— burden with
Enthusi- —— -asm.
Chorus:
Get a —— move, etc.
W'en the —— trouble
Hits yer native land
Take a —— rifle

In yer —— 'and
Keep yer —— upper lip
Stiff as stiff kin be,
An' speed a —— bullet for
Pos- —— -terity.

Chorus:

Get a —— move, etc.
W'en the —— bugle
Sounds "Ad- —— -vance"
Don't be like a flock uv sheep
In a —— trance
Biff the —— foeman
Where it don't agree.
Spifler- —— -cate him
To Eternity.

Chorus:

Get a —— move, etc.
Fellers of Australier,
Cobbers, chaps an' mates,
Hear the —— enermy
Kickin' at the gates!
Blow the —— bugle,
Beat the —— drum,
Upper-cut and out the cow
To kingdom- —— -come!
Chorus:
Get a —— move on,
Have some —— sense.
Learn the —— art of
Self de- —— -fence!

AN OLD MASTER

We were cartin' lathes and palin's from the slopes of Mount St. Leonard,
With our axles near the road-bed and the mud as stiff as glue;
And our bullocks weren't precisely what you'd call conditioned nicely,
And meself and Messmate Mitchell had our doubts of gettin' through.

It had rained a tidy skyful in the week before we started,
But our tucker-bag depended on the sellin' of our load;
So we punched 'em on by inches, liftin' 'em across the pinches,
Till we struck the final section of the worst part of the road.

We were just congratulatin' one another on the journey,
When we blundered in a pot-hole right within the sight of goal,
Where the bush-track joins the metal. Mitchell, as he saw her settle,
Justified his reputation at the peril of his soul.

We were in a glue-pot, certain —- red and stiff and most tenacious;
Over naves and over axles —- waggon sittin' on the road.
"'Struth," says I, "they'll never lift her. Take a shot from Hell to shift her.
Nothin' left us but unyoke 'em and sling off the blessed load."

Now, beside our scene of trouble stood a little one-roomed humpy,
Home of an enfeebled party by the name of Dad McGee.
William was, I pause to mention, livin' on an old-age pension
Since he gave up bullock-punchin' at the age of eighty-three.

Startled by our exclamations, Daddy hobbled from the shanty,
Hobbled out and over to us on his old rheumatic pins,
Shadin' his old eyes and peerin' here and there around the clearin',
While we watched his consternation with half-sympathetic grins.

"Eh! Wot's happened now?" he quavered, in a weak and shaky treble,

Gazin' where the stranded waggon looked like some half-foundered ship.
Then the state o' things he spotted, "Looks," he says, "like you was potted,"
And he toddled up to Mitchell. "Here," said he, "gimme that whip."

Mitchell, bein' out o' patience, flung a glance of anger at him,
Followed by some fancy language of his very choicest brand.
Then old daddy seemed to straighten. "Now," he yelled, "don't keep me waitin'!
Pass that whip, you blarsted blue-tongue!" Mitchell put it in his hand.

Well! I've heard of transformations; heard of fellers sort of changin'
In the face of sudden danger or some great emergency;
Heard the like in song and story and in bush traditions hoary,
But I nearly dropped me bundle as I looked at Dad McGee.

While we gazed he seemed to toughen; as his fingers gripped the handle
His old form grew straight and supple, and a light leaped in his eye;
And he stepped around the waggon, not with footsteps weak and laggin',
But with firm, determined carriage, as he flung the whip on high.

Now he swung the leaders over, while the whip-lash snarled and volleyed;
And they answered like one bullock, strainin' to each crack and clout;
But he kept his cursin' under, till old Brindle made a blunder;
Then I thought all Hell had hit me, and the master opened out.

And the language! Oh, the language! I have known some noble cursers --
"Hell-fire" Mac and "Cursin': Brogan -- men of boundless blasphemee,
Full of fancy exclamations, trimmed with frills and declarations;
But their talk was childish prattle to that language of McGee.

In a trance stood messmate Mitchell; seemed to me I must be dreamin';
While the wondrous words and phrases only genius could loose
Roared and rumbled fast and faster in the throat of that Old Master —-

Oaths and curses tipped with lightning, cracklin' flames of fierce abuse.

Then we knew the man before us was a Master of our callin';
One of those great lords of language gone for ever from Outback;
Heroes of an ancient order; men who punched across the border;
Vanished giants of the 'sixties; puncher-princes of the track.

Now we heard the timbers strainin', heard the waggon's loud complainin',
And the master cried triumphant, as he swung 'em into line,
As they put their toes into it, lifted her, and pulled her through it:
"That's the way we useter do it in the days o' sixty-nine!"

Near the foot of Mount St. Leonard lives an old, enfeebled party
Who retired from bullock-punchin' at the age of eighty-three.
If you seek him folk will mention, merely, that he draws the pension;
But to us he looms a Master -- Prince of Punchers, Dad McGee!

THE LONG ROAD HOME

When I go back from Billy's place I always have to roam
The mazy road, the crazy road that leads the long way home.
Ma always says, "Why don't you come through Mr Donkin's land?
The footbridge track will bring you back." Ma doesn't understand.
I cannot go that way, you know, because of Donkin's dog;
So I set forth and travel north,, and cross the fallen log.

Last week, when I was coming by, that log had lizards in it;
And you can't say I stop to play if I just search a minute.
I look around upon the ground and, if there are no lizards,
I go right on and reach the turn in front of Mrs Blizzard's.
I do not seek to cross the creek, because it's deep and floody,
And Ma would be annoyed with me if I came home all muddy.

Perhaps I throw a stone or so at Mrs Blizzard's tank,
Because it's great when I aim straight to hear the stone go "Plank
Then west I wend from Blizzard's Bend, and not a moment wait,
Except, perhaps, at Mr Knapp's, to swing upon his gate.
So up the hill I go, until I reach the little paddock
That Mr Jones at present owns and rents to Mr Craddock.

For boys my size the sudden rise is quite a heavy pull,
And yet I fear a short-cut here because of Craddock's bull;
So I just tease the bull till he's as mad as he can get,
And then I face the corner place that's been so long to let.
It's very well for Ma to tell about my dawdling habits.
What would you do, suppose you knew the place was thick with rabbits?

I do not stay for half a day, as Ma declares I do,.
No, not for more than half-an-hour - perhaps an hour - or two.
Then down the drop I run, slip-slop, where all the road is slithy.

And have to go quite close, you know, to Mr Horner's smithy.
A moment I might tarry by the fence to watch them hammer,
And, I must say, learn more that way than doing sums and grammar.

And, if I do sometimes climb through, I do not mean to linger'.
Though I did stay awhile the day Bill Homer burst his finger.
I just stand there to see the pair bang some hot iron thing
And watch Bill Horner swing the sledge and hit the anvil - Bing!
(For Mr Horner and his son are great big brawny fellows:
Both splendid chaps!) And then, perhaps, they let me blow the bellows.

A while I stop beside the shop, and talk to Mr Horner;
Then off I run, and race like fun around by Duggan's Corner.
It's getting late, and I don't wait beside the creek a minute,
Except to stop, maybe, and drop a few old pebbles in it.
A few yards more, and here's the store that's kept by Mr Whittle-
And you can't say I waste the day if I 'ust wait… a little.

One day, you know, a year ago, a man gave me a penny,
And Mr Whittle sold me sweets (but not so very many).
You never know your luck, and so I look to see what's new
In Mr Whittle's window.There's a peppermint or two,
Some buttons and tobacco (Mr Whittle calls it "baccy"),
And fish in tins, and tape, and pins…. And then a voice calls, "Jacky!"

"I'm coming, Ma.I've been so far-around by Duggan's Corner.
I had to stay awhile to say 'Good day' to Mr Horner.
I feel so fagged; I've tramped and dragged through mud and over logs, Ma -
I could not go short-cuts, you know, because of bulls and dogs, Ma.
The creek, Ma? Why, it's very high ! You don't call that a gutter?
Bill Horner chews tobacco, Ma…. I'd like some bread and butter."

THE TRIANTIWONTIGONGOLOPE

There's a very funny insect that you do not often spy,

And it isn't quite a spider, and it isn't quite a fly;

It is something like a beetle, and a little like a bee,

But nothing like a wooly grub that climbs upon a tree.

Its name is quite a hard one, but you'll learn it soon, I hope.

So try:

Tri-

Tri-anti-wonti-

Triantiwontigongolope.

It lives on weeds and wattle-gum, and has a funny face;

Its appetite is hearty, and its manners a disgrace.

When first you come upon it, it will give you quite a scare,

But when you look for it again, you find it isn't there.

And unless you call it softly it will stay away and mope.

So try:

Tri-

Tri-anti-wonti-

Triantiwontigongolope.

It trembles if you tickle it or tread upon its toes;

It is not an early riser, but it has a snubbish nose.

If you snear at it, or scold it, it will scuttle off in shame,

But it purrs and purrs quite proudly if you call it by its name,

And offer it some sandwiches of sealing-wax and soap.

So try:

Tri-

Tri-anti-wonti-

Triantiwontigongolope .

But of course you haven't seen it; and I truthfully confess

That I haven't seen it either, and I don't know its address.
For there isn't such an insect, though there really might have been
If the trees and grass were purple, and the sky was bottle green.
It's just a little joke of mine, which you'll forgive, I hope.
Oh, try!
Tri-
Tri-anti-wonti-
Triantiwontigongolope.

The Looking Glass

When I look into the looking glass
I'm always sure to see -
No matter how I dodge about -
Me, looking out at me.

I often wonder as I look,
And those strange features spy,
If I, in there, think I'm as plain
As I, out here, think I.

THE TRAVELLER

As I rode in to Burrumbeet,
I met a man with funny feet;
And, when I paused to ask him why
His feet were strange, he rolled his eye
And said the rain would spoil the wheat;
So I rode on to Burrumbeet.

As I rode in to Beetaloo,
I met a man whose nose was blue;
And when I asked him how he got
A nose like that, he answered, "What
Do bullocks mean when they say 'Moo'?"
So I rode on to Beetaloo.

As I rode in to Ballarat,
I met a man who wore no hat;
And, when I said he might take cold,
He cried, "The hills are quite as old
As yonder plains, but not so flat."
So I rode on to Ballarat.

As I rode in to Gundagai,
I met a man and passed him by
Without a nod, without a word.
He turned, and said he'd never heard
Or seen a man so wise as I.
But I rode on to Gundagai.

As I rode homeward, full of doubt,
I met a stranger riding out:
A foolish man he seemed to me;
But, "Nay, I am yourself," said he,
"Just as you were when you rode out."
So I rode homeward, free of doubt.

WILLIAM HENRY OGILVIE

Will H. Ogilvie was a Scottish-Australian narrative poet, horseman, jackaroo, and drover. Ogilvie was part of the trio of Australian bush poets, with Banjo Paterson (1864–1941) and Henry Lawson(1867–1922). Wearing the title 'Universally acclaimed in Australia as a bush balladist of the "Outback,"' Will H. Ogilvie wrote over 1,100 poems, including A Scotch night, The Australian, Summer country, Kings of the earth, and Whaup o' the rede. Ogilvie wrote lyrical and romantic poetry noted for its balladic style, with graphic descriptions of Australian Outback life and characters. As he was known, Will also wrote a great deal of work on English and Scottish themes and has been included in collections of English and Scottish poetry. His work was initially published in, and he is most closely associated with, Australia. Before being printed in books, many works in the newspapers were under the pen name of 'Glenrowan' and also 'Swingle-Bar.'

HIS GIPPSLAND GIRL
(1898)

Now, money was scarce and work was slack
And love to his heart Crept in,
And he rode away on the Northern track
To war with the world and win;
And he vowed by the locket upon his breast
And its treasure, one red gold curl,
To work with with a will in the fartherest West
For the sake of his Gippsland girl.

The hot wind blows on the dusty plain
And the red sun burns above,
But he sees her face at his side again,
And he strikes each blow for love.
He toils by the light of one far-off star
For the winning of one white pearl,
And the swinging pick and the driving bar
Strike home for the Gippsland girl.

With an aching wrist and a back that's bent,
With salt sweat blinding eyes,
'Tis little he'd reek if his life were spent
In the winning so grand a prize.
His shear blades flash and over his hand
The folds of the white fleece curl,
And all day long he sticks to his stand
For the love of his Gippsland girl.

When the shearing's done and the shed's cut out
On Barwon and Narran and Bree;
When the shearer mates with the rouseabout
And the Union man with the free;

When the doors of the shanty, open wide,
An uproarious welcome hurl,
He passes by on the other side
For the sake of his gippsland girl.

When summer lay brown on the Western Land
He rode once more to the South,
Athirst for the touch of a lily hand
And the kiss of a rosebud mouth;
And he sang the songs that shorten the way,
And he envied not king or earl,
And he spared not the spur in his dappled grey
For the sake of his Gippsland girl.

At the garden gate when the shadows fell
His hopes in the dusk lay dead;
'Nelli? Oh! Surely you heard that Nell
Is married a month' they said.
He spoke no word; with a dull, dumb pain
At his heart, and his brain awhirl
He turned his grey to the North again
For the sake of his Gippsland girl.

And he rung the board in a Paroo shed
By the sweat of his aching brow,
But he blued his cheque, for he grimly said,
'There is nothing to live for now.'
And out and away where the big floods start
And the Darling dust-showers swirl,
There's a drunken shearer who broke his heart
Over a Gippsland girl!

HIS EPITAPH
(1898)

On a little old bush racecourse at the back of No Man's Land,
Where the mulgas mark the furlongs and a dead log marks the stand,
There's a square of painted railings showing white against the loam
Where they fight for inside running as they round the bend for home;
Just a lonely grave and graveyard that are left to Nature's care,
For the wild bush-flowers that brighten it were never planted there;
No monument or marble that will speak his praise or blame,
No verse to tell his story and no mark to prove his name.
But carved upon the white rail that is weather-worn and thin
Is the simple, roug-hewn legend: HE ALWAS ROD TO WIN!

Some poor, uncared-for jockey-boy, who never earned a name –
It's the boys who "ride to orders" who can find the road to Fame;
And the flowers and marble head-stones and the wealth of gear and gold
Are the prizes of the riders who will "stop them" when they're told!
Just a whisper at the saddling; "He's the only danger, Dan,
That's the boy will try to beat you – stop him, any way you can!"
Just a crowding at the corner and a crossing in the straight,
And a plucky little horseman who is "pulling out" too late;
A heavy fall, a horse is loose – and a lightweight carried in –
A shallow grave, a railing and: "HE ALWAS ROD TO WIN!"

Some brave, brown-handed comrade who has learned the rider's worth
Has carved those rough words o'er him for the eyes of all the earth;
And though few may chance to pass him as he lies in simple state,
Those few will hold him honoured by the friendship of his mate.
And when, in Life's keen struggle, we shall fight for inside place,
When they crowd us at the corner and we drop from out the race,
When the ringing hoofs go forward and the cheering greets the best,
And the prize is for the winner, and the red spurs for the rest,
May we find some true-heart comrade, when they've filled the last clods in,
Who will carve these words above us: HE ALWAS ROD TO WIN!

THE AUSTRALIAN
(1916)

The bravest thing God ever made!

(A British Officer's Opinion)

The skies that arched his land were blue,
His bush-born winds were warm and sweet,
And yet from earliest hours he knew
The tides of victory and defeat:
From fierce floods thundering at his birth,
From red droughts ravening while he played,
He learned no fear no foes on earth -
The bravest thing God ever made!

The bugles of the Motherland
Rang ceaselessly across the sea,
To call him and his lean brown band
To shape Imperial destiny.,
He went by youth's grave purpose willed,
The goal unknown, the cost unweighed,
The promise of his blood fulfilled -
The bravest thing God ever made!

We know - it is our deathless pride! -
The splendour of his first fierce blow;
How, reckless, glorious, undenied,
He stormed those steel-lined cliffs we know!
And none who saw him scale the height
Behind his reeking bayonet blade
Would rob him of his title right -
The bravest thing God ever made!

Bravest, where half a world of men
Are brave beyond all earth's rewards,
So stoutly none shall charge again
Till the last breaking of the swords;
Wounded or hale, won home from war,
Or yonder by the Lone Pine laid,
Give him his due for evermore -
The bravest thing God ever made!

FROM THE GULF

Store cattle from Nelanjie! The mob goes feeding past,
With half-a-mile of sandhill 'twixt the leaders and the last;
The nags that move behind them are the good old Queensland stamp-
Short backs and perfect shoulders that are priceless on a camp;
And these are men that ride them, broad-cheated, tanned, and tall,
The bravest hearts amongst us and the lightest hands of all:
Oh, let them wade in Wonga grass and taste the Wonga dew,
And let them spread, those thousand head-for we've been droving tool

Store cattle from Nelanjie! By half-a-hundred towns,
By northern ranges rough and red, by rolling open downs
By stock-routes brown and burnt and bare, by floodwrapped river-bends,
They've hunted them from gate to gate-the drover has no friends!
But idly they may ride to-day beneath the scorching sun
And let the hungry bullocks try the grass on Wonga run;
No overseer will dog them here to "see the cattle through,"
But they may spread their thousand head-for we've been droving too!

Store cattle from Nelanjie! They've a naked track to steer;
The stockyards at Wodonga are a long way down from here;
The creeks won't run till God knows when, and half the holes are dry;
The tanks are few and far between and water's dear to buy:
There's plenty at the Brolga bore for all his stock and mine-
We'll pass him with a brave God-speed across the Border Line;
And if he goes a five-mile stage and loiters slowly through,
We'll only think the more of him-for we've been droving too I

Store cattle from Nelanjie! They're mute as milkers now;
But yonder grizzled drover, with the care-lines on his brow,
Could tell of merry musters on the big Nelanjie plains,
With blood upon the chestnut's flanks and foam upon the reins;

Could tell of nights upon the road when those same mild-eyed steers
Went ringing round the river bend and through the scrub like spears;
And if his words are rude and rough, we know his words are true,
We know what wild Nelanjies are-and we've been droving too !

Store cattle from Nelanjie! Around the fire at night
They've watched the pine-tree shadows lift before the dancing light;
They've lain awake to listen when the weird bushvoices speak,
And heard the lilting bells go by along the empty creek;
They've spun the yarns of hut and camp, the tales of play and work,
The wondrous tales that gild the road from Normanton to Bourke;
They've told of fortunes foul and fair, of women false and true,
And well we know the songs they've sung-for we've been droving too!

Store cattle from Nelanjie! Their breath is on the breeze;
You hear them tread, a thousand head, in blue-grass to the knees;
The lead is on the netting-fence, the wings are spreading wide,
The lame and laggard scarcely move so slow the drovers ride!
But let them stay and feed to-day for sake of Auld Lang Syne;
They'll never get a chance like this below the Border Iodine;
And if they tread our frontage down, what's that to me or you?
What's ours to fare, by God they'll shared for we've been droving tool

LEILA.

THE nodding plumes steal slowly by;
Fair women turn their heads aside ;
And yet the purest there must die
As poor Love-Leila died.

In town, a boy who never knew

Of better love than this
Is mourning Leila's eyes of blue,

And lone for Leila's kiss.

A horseman on the burning plains

A hundred miles north-west
Bends gently o'er his bridle-reins

And prays for Leila, Rest!

A man who buried all his dreams

Of Love long years ago,
Has dropped one other tear where gleams

Love-Leila's breast of snow.

All virtuous the world appears :

But those who turn aside
May never win such honest tears

As fell when Leila died.

A DREAMER OF DREAMS.

THE song-thrush loves the laurel,
The stone-chat haunts the broom.
But the seagull must have room
Where the white drift spins ashore

And the winds and waters quarrel
With the old hate evermore.

You clear with scythe or sabre
A pathway for your feet,
I move in meadow sweet
By the side of silent streams.

And you are lord of labour
And I am serf of dreams.

You fill the red wine flagon
And drink and ride away
To the toil of each new day,
But I quaff till dawn be pale

To the knight or dame or dragon
Of a dream-^spun fairy tale.

You win your chosen maiden
With a bracelet for her wrist ;
Lightly courted, lightly kissed.
She is yours for weal or woe,

But my heart goes sorrow-laden
For a dream-love long ago.

Let our pathways part for ever,
I am all content with mine —
For when lips are tired of wine
As the long-dead dreamers tell,

There are poppies by the river.

There is hemlock in the dell

BALLADE OF WINDY NIGHTS.

HAVE you learnt the sorrow of windy nights
When lilacs down in the garden moan,
And stars are flickering faint, wan lights,
And voices whisper in wood and stone ?
When steps on the stairway creak and groan,
And shadowy ghosts take an hour of ease

In dim-lit galleries all their own ?
Do you know the sorrow of nights like these ?

Have you Iain awake on the windy nights

Slighted by sleep and to rest unknown,
When keen remorse is a whip that smites

With every gust on the window blown ?

When phantom Love from a broken throne
Steps down through the Night's torn tapestries.

Sad-eyed and wistful, and ah ! so lone?
Do you know the sorrow of nights like these ?

Have you felt a touch on the windy nights —

The touch of a hand not flesh nor bone,
But a mystical something, pale, that plights

With waning stars and with dead stars strown ?

Or heard grey lips with the fire all flown

Pleading again in a lull o' the breeze —

A long life's wreck in a short hour shown ?
Do you know the sorrow of nights like these ?

Ah, the whirimnd reaped where a wind is sown,
And the phantom Love in the night one sees !

Ah, the touching hand and the pleading tone!
Do you know the sorrow of nights like these ?

THE CRUELLEST DREAM.

SO here at the last I find
I am holding again your hand,
And why you are cruel no more, but kind,
I scarcely can understand ;
But I know that the earth is ablaze with roses,

I know that the lilies make paths for our feet.
And as long as your hand on my own hand closes
I know that you love me, sweet !

I hear as of old your voice

That is speaking my name so low, so low,
Till all things living rejoice

And all things gladden that grow ;
And I know that the skies are a dazzling blue

And the face of the earth is fair,
And 1 know that the birds are calling you true

In songs that are everywhere.

I am kissing you over and over,

I am holding you close to my heart,
As of old we are lover and lover

And live in a world apart . . .
/ hear no longer your sweet voice calling.

But only the waU of the wind instead ;
I have lost your face in the shadows falling —

Darling! the cruellest dream is dead.

ADA CAMBRIDGE

Ada Cambridge, later known as Ada Cross, was an English-born Australian writer. She wrote more than 25 works of fiction, three volumes of poetry, and two autobiographical works. Many of her novels were serialized in Australian newspapers but have never been published in book form. Although not financially successful as a poet – her collections were often self-published and sold poorly. The vast majority of her literary talent is seen in her verse rather than her prose, which, though lively and entertaining, was primarily written for an everyday newspaper audience. As she grew older, Cambridge's poetry changed from religious and romantic subjects to more radical ones that increasingly showed a feminist perspective on life. It provided a vital snapshot of many women in late 19th century Australia that is still popular today.

CRAVEN-HEART

Those anguished voices in the air!
Oh, I could shriek and tear my hair
In rage, rebellion and despair.

But what is one, amid a throng
So vast and merciless and strong,
To make attempt to right the wrong?

What ear would hear me if I cried?
And who would rally to my side?
What could I do to stem the tide?

Though I should plunge in flood and flame,
And suffer every shame and blame,
The world would triumph all the same.

I am not called upon to pay.
So why join in the hopeless fray,
And waste my brief and precious day?

"AFTER OUR LIKENESS"

Before me now a little picture lies—
A little shadow of a childish face,
Childishly sweet, yet with the dawning grace
Of thought and wisdom on her lips and eyes.

Fair, oval, broad-brow'd face—small, delicate head—
Transparent skin, with blue veins shining through—
All the soft outlines, beautiful and true,
Bring me the echo of the words "God said."

Made "in our image"—sure 'tis that we see,
God's likeness, in the fair face of a child,
By the world's sin and passion undefiled—
Ay, as I look, it seems quite plain to me.

The light wherein the little features shine,
Strange, mystic light, so undefined and faint,
So far too pure for any words to paint—
'Tis a reflection of the Face divine.

Some day the earthly shadows will be cast
Across that sunshine—it may be to dim
Awhile the visible countenance of Him;
But 'twill be there—the likeness—to the last.

Some day the lucid waters, in which lie
Pictured those glorious lineaments, will be
Stirred up and troubled like a stormy sea;—
But they will yet re-settle—by-and-by.

They will re-settle when the soul is still'd,

Its passions, its wild longings, and its pain;
The pure reflection will shine out again
When earth's hopes are relinquish'd, unfulfill'd.

They will re-settle in those after-years
When life's hard lessons have been conned and learn'd;
When this child's beauty will have all return'd,
More lovely for the trouble and the tears.

They will re-settle in the calm of death,
When the sweet eyes are laid asleep, and when
The heart is hush'd. Truly God's likeness then—
The mirror clear, unsullied by a breath.

Ah! while I look, and trace each tender line,
I think most of the day when I shall see
The dear face in that perfect purity,
Its mortal features clothed with the divine.

This self-same face, but with the image bright,
Nevermore undefined, and faint, and dim;
This self-same face, yet like the face of Him,
In glory and in beauty infinite.

"THIS ENLIGHTENED AGE"

A Meditation in the British Museum.

I say it to myself—in meekest awe
Of Progress, electricity and steam,
Of this almighty age—this liberal age,
That has no time to breathe, or think, or dream,—

I ask it of myself, with bated breath,
Casting a furtive glance about the hall,—
Our fathers, were their times so very dark?
Were they benighted heathens after all?

Had they not their Galileo—Newton too—
And men as great, though not a Stephenson?
Had they not passable scholars in fair Greece,
Who traced the paths we deign to walk upon
Had they not poets in those dismal days—
Homer and Shakespeare, and a few between?
Had they not rulers in their barbarous states,
Who scattered laws for our wise hands to glean?

Had they not painters, who knew how to paint—
Raphael, to take an instance—well as we,
With near four hundred years of light the less?
Is Phidias matched in our great century?

And architects? Sure Egypt, and old Rome,
And ruined Athens tell of fair reputes!
The Pyramids, and temples of the Greeks,
May vie with our town-halls and institutes.

Their marble Venice, with her dappled tints,
Their grey old minsters, strong as chiselled rocks,
Their Tyrolean castles, lifted high,
May outlast all our brick-and-mortar blocks.
And were there not refinements in those days,
And elegant luxuries of domestic life?
I read the answer in the precious things
Whereof these clustering cabinets are rife.

What can we show so beautiful in art?
What new of ours can match their wondrous old?—
This fragile porcelain—this Venetian glass—
This delicate necklace of Etruscan gold.

And was there not religion—when the Church
Was one—a common mother—loved and feared?
When haughty souls rejoiced to bear her yoke?
When all those grand monastic piles were reared?

And were there not some preachers—Chrysostoms,
Whose golden words still linger, like a chime
Of falling echoes in lone alpine glens,
Amongst the sonorous voices of our time?
And soldiers—heroes? Do we shame them much?
Have men more courage than in days of yore?
Are they more jealous for their manhood now?
Do they respect and honour women more?

Are they more noble than those good old knights,
Who scorned to strike a foe save in the face—
Who reckoned gold as dross to gallant deeds,
And counted death far happier than disgrace?

Is life more grand with us, who bask at ease,

And count that only excellent which pays,

Than 'twas to the stout hearts that wore the steel

In those dark, turbulent, fearless, fighting days?

*

O nineteenth century! God has given you light;

The morning has been spreading—that is all.

O liberal age! stoop your conceited head,

And gather up the crumbs that they let fall.

A SIGH IN THE NIGHT

O sweet darkness, still, and calm, and lonely!
Spread thy downy pinions round about.
Spare me from thy hidden riches only
One dream-face; blot all the others out.

Bring him now, for thou hast power to free him,
From that ugly garb he wears by day;
Bring him now—my darling!—let me see him
Ere the tender kindness pass away.

O sweet night-winds, wandering in the larches!
Sigh, and croon, and whisper as you creep;
Sing my songs through green cathedral arches,
While the weary workers are asleep.
Snarl and fret not of the grief and passion;
Sing in minor cadence, sweet and low;
Sing of peace and rest, in soft wind-fashion—
Of the love and faith I used to know!

THE END